Table of Contents

Park Map 4
Introduction 7
Chapter 1: Hikes Near Black Rock Campground . . 9
  1 High View Nature Trail 10
  2 South Park Peak 12
  3 Short Loop 13
  4 Eureka Peak 15
  33 CRH: Black Rock to Covington Flats 84
  34 CRH: Covington Flats to Keys View Road . . 86
Chapter 2: Hikes Near Indian Cove Campground . . 19
  5 Indian Cove Nature Trail 20
  6 Boy Scout Trail 22
  7 Fortynine Palms Oasis 25
  8 Oasis of Mara (Twentynine Palms Oasis) . . . 28
Chapter 3: Hikes Near Lost Horse Valley Campgrounds 29
  6 Boy Scout Trail 22
  9 North View / Maze / Window Rock Loop . . . 31
  10 Hidden Valley Nature Trail 35
  11 Barker Dam Nature Trail 37
  12 Wonderland Ranch Wash 39
  13 Juniper Flats 41
  14 Stubbe Spring Loop 44
  15 Lost Horse Mine 47
  16 Keys View Loop 49
  17 Inspiration Peak 50
  18 Cap Rock Nature Trail 52
  19 Ryan Ranch Homestead 54
  20 Ryan Mountain 56
  34 CRH: Covington Flats to Keys View Road . . 86
  35 CRH: Keys View Rd to Geology Tour Rd . . 89
Chapter 4: Hikes Near Queen Valley Campgrounds . 58
  21 Luck Boy Vista 60
  22 Desert Queen Mine 62

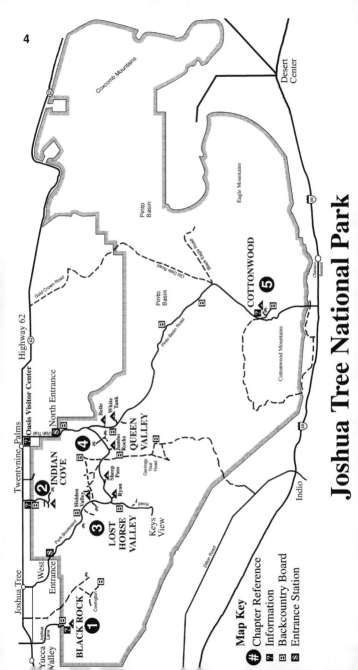

4

Joshua Tree National Park

Map Key

Chapter Reference
ℹ Information
B Backcountry Board
S Entrance Station

23 Pine City 63
24 Skull Rock Nature Trail 66
25 Split Rock Loop 68
26 Arch Rock Nature Trail 70
27 Cholla Cactus Garden 72
35 CRH: Keys View Rd to Geology Tour Rd . . 89
36 CRH: Geology Tour Rd to Pinto Basin Rd . . 91
37 CRH: Pinto Basin Road to North Entrance . . 92
Chapter 5: Hikes Near Cottonwood Campground . 73
28 Cottonwood Spring Nature Trail 74
29 Mastodon Peak Loop 76
30 Moorten's Mill / Little Chilcoot 78
31 Lost Palms Oasis 79
32 Bajada Nature Trail 82
Chapter 6: California Riding & Hiking Trail 83
33 Black Rock to Covington Flats 84
34 Covington Flats to Keys View Road 86
35 Keys View Road to Geology Tour Road 89
36 Geology Tour Road to Pinto Basin Road 91
37 Pinto Basin Road to North Entrance 92
Mileage Chart 94
About the Author / Other Books by Author 96

Map Key (For topographical and line maps)

- 🇹 **Trailhead**
- ▲ **Campground**
- ⛆ **Picnic Area**
- 🛈 **Ranger Station/Information**
- − − − **Featured Trails**
- ‑ ‑ ‑ ‑ **Other Trails**
- ▬▬▬ **Paved Roads**
- ▬·▬ **Dirt Roads**
- • • • • **Day Use Area Boundary**
- **#** **Mileage Points**
- **(#)** **Hike Reference Numbers (line maps)**

HIDDEN VALLEY TRAIL

THE NATURAL FEATURES OF THIS
ROCK ENCLOSED VALLEY ARE
MARKED BY TRAILSIDE SIGNS
AROUND THE OUTSIDE LOOP.
WALKING TIME IS ABOUT ONE
HOUR FOR THE ONE MILE TRAIL.

YOU ARE
HERE

← START OF TRAIL

Introduction

Joshua Tree National Park, located in the heart of southern California, is one of this country's national treasures. This park was established to protect representative portions of both the Mojave and the Colorado deserts. The best way to explore and enjoy these two different deserts is by traveling on foot. Walk the trails and see the desert's abounding life, its colorful history, and subtle, yet sometimes profound beauty. Read the different hike descriptions in this book to learn about the interesting history, geology, scenery, plants, and animals of the park.

Hike, explore, and enjoy Joshua Tree National Park!

About This Guide

This book describes the official park trails. The hikes are grouped in chapters based around campground areas. Use the park map (page 4) to help choose the chapter for a particular area. The mileage chart at the back of the book will assist in selecting a hike tailored to your time, mileage, or difficulty preferences.

Each hike description is preceded by a list of pertinent facts. The list includes the elevation difference between the highest and lowest point on the trail and the approximate amount of uphill travel between the beginning and end of the hike.

Elevation profiles show elevation changes in relation to mileage. Topographical maps highlight the featured trail with mile indicators, connecting trails, roads, points of interest, day use boundaries, and any nearby facilities.

Six symbols, placed next to hike titles, provide quick information about the trail. Symbol meanings are as follows:

10 This trail is one of the top ten in the park. Selection is based upon popularity of a trail, the variety of highlights and points of interest, and the author's opinion.

Signs or pamphlets explain highlights along the trail.

Children should enjoy this trail. There are highlights to keep a child interested throughout the hike. Mileage and difficulty were considered for this designation.

Backcountry camping is allowed on this hike.

Horses and other stock animals are allowed on the trail.

Bicycles are allowed on at least a portion of the trail.

Cautions, Tips, and Regulations

- Protective Clothing: A hat, sunglasses, and sunscreen are recommended to protect against the bright desert sun. Prepare for temperature extremes between day and night.
- Water: Carry at least one gallon of water per day per hiker.
- Mines: All mine shafts and associated buildings should be considered unsafe for entry.
- Flash Floods: Flash floods may occur during periods of heavy rain. To avoid encountering this danger, don't camp or hike in canyons and washes during rainy periods.
- Stock Animals: These animals are only allowed on trails designated for stock use. They are not allowed to graze on vegetation or drink from park water sources.
- Backcountry Camping: Overnight users must register at a self-registration backcountry board. These boards are marked on the park map (page 4). Camps must be located one mile from the road, 500 feet from the trail, and outside day use areas.
- For additional information contact Joshua Tree National Park, 74485 National Park Drive, Twentynine Palms, CA 92277, (760) 367-5500. For campground reservations, call 1-800-365-2267. Website: www.nps.gov/jotr

Chapter 1
Hikes Near Black Rock Campground

Black Rock Campground is in the northwest corner of the park. The campground sits at the mouth of a canyon surrounded by high hills. This part of the park is thick with High Desert vegetation. Large Joshua trees grow in dense concentrations. Junipers, pines, cacti, and a variety of desert shrubs are some other common plants found on the hillsides surrounding the campground.

Facilities at Black Rock include a visitor center and a 100-site campground with running water and flush toilets. There is a campground fee and sites can be reserved. The nearest town is Yucca Valley, five miles away.

To reach Black Rock, take Joshua Lane south from Highway 62 in Yucca Valley. Follow the signs for the campground. (See Chapter 6 for two additional trails in the area.)

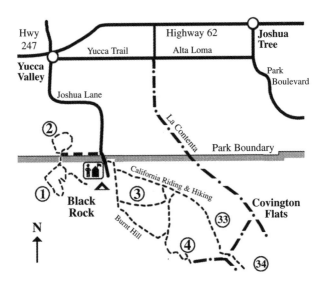

1 High View Nature Trail

Highlights: interpretive trail, high scenic vistas
Mileage: 1.3 mile loop, (2.3 mile loop from campground)
Time: 1 hour (1.5 hours)
Difficulty: moderate   **Map:** Trail Map 1
Elevation Difference: 355'   **Total Uphill Travel:** 365'
Use Restrictions: day use only, no horses or bicycles
Access: South Park Parking Area. Follow the dirt road that leads west immediately before the entrance to Black Rock Campground. Travel to the parking lot at the end of the road.

Elevation Profile

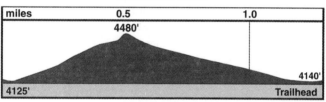

miles	0.5	1.0

4480'

4140'

4125'   Trailhead

Description: This moderately steep trail leads to a good viewpoint of the town of Yucca Valley and Mt. San Gorgonio, an 11,499' peak located in the San Bernardino Mountains. Mt. San Gorgonio, with its winter mantle of snow, provides a beautiful contrast with the desert mountains that surround High View.

Take advantage of the benches located at several points along the trail. Rest, enjoy the scenery, and study the varied vegetation of the Mojave Desert. Watch lizards and small animals scurry around.

Numbered posts point out the highlights along the trail. Obtain the corresponding interpretive handout at the Black Rock Visitor Center. The handout provides interesting information on plant adaptations in a high desert environment and explains animal relationships with these plants.

The loop is designed for clockwise travel. From the parking lot, the trail leads over a short flat section before beginning the steady 355' ascent to the ridgetop. There is a trail register and bench at the high point on the trail. The equally steady descent leads down a drainage to gentler ground. The last 1/4 mile is fairly level.

The nature trail can also be accessed from Black Rock Campground. A spur trail, which begins west of the ranger station, travels 1/2 mile along the base of the hills. It intersects the nature trail 150 yards south of the parking lot.

Trail Map 1

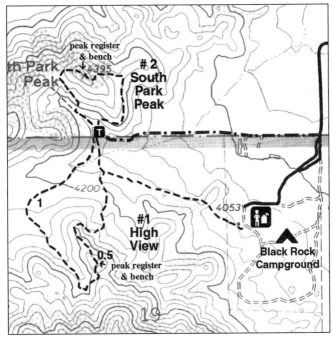

USGS Topographical Map: Yucca Valley South 7.5'

2 South Park Peak (4395')

Highlights: interpretive trail, summit with good views
Mileage: 0.7 mile loop   **Time:** < 1 hour
Difficulty: moderate   **Map:** Trail Map 1
Elevation Difference: 255'   **Total Uphill Travel:** 284'
Use Restrictions: day use only, no horses or bicycles
Access: South Park Parking Area. Follow the dirt road that leads
west immediately before the entrance to Black Rock Campground.
Travel to the parking lot at the end of the road.

Elevation Profile

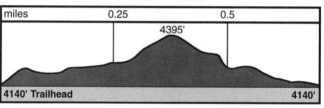

Description: This short loop trail is located outside the park.
However, its proximity to Black Rock Campground makes it
worthy of inclusion in this book. The Yucca Valley Parks
District maintains this trail. The hike was chosen as a "kid
pick" because it is short. With a little effort, children can reach
a summit giving them a sense of accomplishment.

The trail leads a short distance to the top of a peak that sits
on the edge of the Morongo Basin. From the summit, there are
unobstructed views of the town of Yucca Valley, views across
to the San Bernardino Mountains, and views back into the park
interior. A bench located at the summit provides a good spot to
sit and enjoy the views or a spectacular desert sunset.

There are several interpretive signs along the trail. Take a
few minutes to learn about the plants of the Mojave Desert.

Read about the special plant and animal relationships and early Indian uses of these plants. Sign the summit register.

3 Short Loop

Highlights: elevated views; variety of vegetation including large Joshua trees, junipers, and pines; 1992 earthquake crevice

Mileage: 4 mile loop	**Time:** 2-3 hours
Difficulty: moderate	**Map:** Trail Map 2
Elevation Difference: 522'	**Total Uphill Travel:** 619'

Use Restrictions: no bicycles

Access: Black Rock Trailhead. Look for a large signboard on the east side of the road, just inside the campground entrance. There is limited parking at the trailhead; however, there's additional parking at the ranger station just up the road.

Elevation Profile

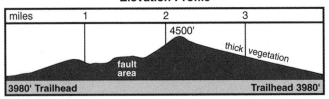

Description: The Short Loop provides a variety of terrain, vegetation, and views. The trail passes through hills, washes, ravines, and valleys. It travels over ridges and a low pass between two mountains. The vegetation is particularly thick and noteworthy on the latter portion of the hike. Many large pinyon pines, oaks, and junipers are interspersed with the more typical vegetation of the Mojave Desert such as black brush, yuccas, and Joshua trees. A short section of the loop known as the Fault Trail travels near a crevice believed to be the result

of the 1992 Landers earthquake (magnitude 7.6). In places, the crevice is about one foot wide and up to three feet deep.

The first half of the trail follows the Eureka Peak trail (hike #4). From the trailhead, travel a short distance east to a wide wash. Turn right and hike up the wash about 150 yards. At this point, the trail exits the wash to the left (east). A large sign indicates the California Riding and Hiking Trail. Follow this trail through low rolling hills for 1.2 miles. Look for a fork in the trail marked with a post or sign for the Fault Trail, "FT." Take the right fork.

From the fork, the Fault Trail travels steeply up and down over rolling ridges. The best place to view the earthquake fault is on a flat ridge plateau about 0.2 miles from the fork. Walk east of the trail 120'. A visible crevice parallels the trail for about 60'.

The trail descends the ridge and passes two trail junctions for Eureka Peak. Continue following the Short Loop trail markers. The trail leads up a bushy wash, through a narrow gully, then steeply up to a pass. The descent from the pass is more gradual. While hiking down from the pass, take note of

USGS Topographical Maps: Yucca Valley South, Joshua Tree S. 7.5'

and enjoy the beautiful High Desert vegetation. It is both plentiful and varied on this section of the hike. The large distant mountain that looms over the valley is Mt. San Gorgonio. It's usually snow capped through much of the year.

The trail descends to Black Rock Canyon Wash. Turn right (north) and travel down the wash and back to the trailhead.

4   **Eureka Peak**

Highlights: peak with great views; varied terrain—wide desert washes to steep narrow canyons to ridgetops; variety of vegetation including large pinyons and Joshua trees

Mileage: 5 miles (one-way)   **Time:** 3 - 4 hours

Difficulty: moderately strenuous (uphill)   **Map:** Trail Map 3

Elevation Difference: 1538'   **Total Uphill Travel:** 1631'

Use Restrictions: no bicycles

Access: Black Rock Trailhead. Look for a large signboard on the east side of the road, just inside the campground entrance. There is limited parking at the trailhead; however, there's additional parking at the ranger station just up the road.

Finish: Eureka Peak Parking Area. Head east from Yucca Valley on Hwy 62. Turn right (south) on La Contenta Road. Cross Yucca Trail/Alta Loma and continue on a dirt road. Follow the dirt road to a junction on the left side of the road (2.8 miles from Hwy 62). Turn left and drive 5.9 miles to a junction. Turn right. Continue to another junction and turn right. Follow the road to the end.

Elevation Profile

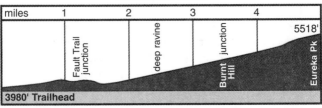

Description: Access to this trail is from either Black Rock or Covington Flats. This dual access allows the option of either a one-way or round-trip hike starting from either direction. The route is described from Black Rock to Covington; the excellent views from the peak are the goal and reward of this five-mile hike. Consider making a round-trip hike. Hiking in the reverse direction usually gives a new perspective. Options for round-trip hikes are provided below.

The route travels through the hills overlooking Yucca Valley, up a wash, into a narrow canyon, over pine covered ridges, then up to the summit. The view from the summit includes Mt. San Jacinto, Mt. San Gorgonio, and the Coachella Valley. The view of Mt. San Jacinto towering almost 10,000' above the floor of the Coachella Valley is particularly breathtaking. Winter snows frequently cap both Mt. San Jacinto and Mt. San Gorgonio. This provides a spectacular contrast with the surrounding desert valley.

The trail leads a short distance east from the trailhead to a wide wash. Turn right and travel up the wash about 150 yards. At this point, the trail exits the wash to the left (east). A large sign identifies the California Riding and Hiking Trail. Follow this trail through low rolling hills for about 1.5 miles. Pass the trail junction for Fault Trail. (There may be a post with the markings "FT.") A short distance farther, the trail enters a major wash. A sign marks the departure of the Eureka Peak trail from the California Riding and Hiking Trail.

Make a sharp right and head south up the wash through a narrow canyon. Soon after exiting the canyon, the wash passes by two trail junctions for the Short Loop and Fault Trail. Stay in the wash following posts and signs marked with "EP" for Eureka Peak.

Close to the halfway point, the wash winds through a beautiful, deep narrow ravine. Large pinyon pines grow from the high rocky sides of the canyon. About a mile after exiting the deep canyon, the wash forks. At this point, there should be a post marking the departure of a horse trail "BF."

Trail Map 3

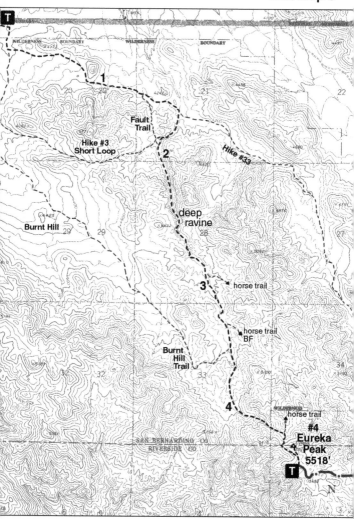

USGS Topographical Maps: Yucca Valley South,
Joshua Tree South 7.5'

Take the right fork and follow the wash to its end in a shallow gully. The trail may occasionally leave the wash to skirt obstructions. From the gully, the trail leads up to the left and over a ridge. About 100 yards beyond the ridgetop, another horse trail departs and heads north (left). This junction may not be marked. Follow the trail that leads in a southerly direction. The trail continues up to a pass then rolls along a mountainside to reach a saddle between Eureka Peak Parking Area and the summit. At this saddle, head left 150 yards to the summit or right 100 yards to the parking area.

Note: Between Black Rock Campground and Eureka Peak, there is a spider web of horse trails. Some of these trails are signed while others may not be. To avoid confusion, carry a map and compass in case trail markers are missing.

Round-Trip Options

Return via Short Loop: Mileage for return via the Short Loop is about 10 miles round-trip. See hike #3 for a description.

Return via Burnt Hill: Mileage for return via Burnt Hill is about 9.75 miles round-trip. Look for the Burnt Hill trail junction around mile 3.5 on the Eureka Peak trail. This trail climbs a short distance from the Eureka Peak Wash to a pass. The remainder of the trail travels gradually downhill through an open valley and past a hill burnt over in the 1970's. The trail intersects Black Rock Canyon Wash. Travel north (right) down the wash and back to the trailhead.

Chapter 2
Hikes Near Indian Cove Campground

Indian Cove Campground is nestled among large boulder piles on the park's north boundary. These boulders are part of the Wonderland of Rocks—a maze of massive monzogranite rock formations extending over twelve square miles. (See hike #18 for geologic details.) Since Indian Cove is generally warmer and more sheltered than other parts of the park, it is popular during the winter.

Facilities at Indian Cove include a ranger station, picnic area, a 101-site campground and a separate 13-site group campground. Both campgrounds are on a reservation system and there is a fee. Campgrounds have tables, fire grates, and vault toilets. Water is available at the ranger station, two miles away. The nearest town with shopping facilities is Twentynine Palms, nine miles away.

To reach Indian Cove, follow Highway 62. Turn south on Indian Cove Road—nine miles east of Joshua Tree (town) or six miles west of Twentynine Palms.

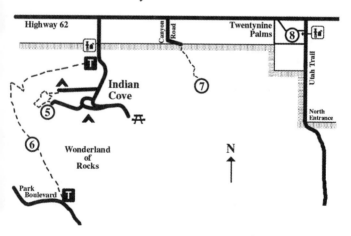

5 Indian Cove Nature Trail

Highlights: interpretive trail, Wonderland of Rocks, Mojave Desert wash, introduction to desert bighorn habitat

Mileage: 0.6 mile loop   **Time:** < 1 hour

Difficulty: easy   **Map:** Trail Map 4

Elevation Difference: relatively level

Use Restrictions: day use only, no horses or bicycles

Access: west end of Indian Cove Campground. Follow the picture signs for the Nature Trail.

Description: This trail skirts the edge of the Wonderland of Rocks and travels through low hills and a wide sandy wash. Signs along the way identify plants, explain plant uses by early Indians, discuss plant and animal relationships, and touch on the natural life of a Mojave Desert wash. The trail is relatively level; however, it drops a short distance to the wash. It follows the wash down about 1/4 mile before ascending a short banking up to higher ground.

While traveling the trail, note the rugged terrain of the Wonderland, particularly to the south of Indian Cove. This is prime desert bighorn sheep habitat. Desert bighorn, a rare subspecies of bighorn sheep, survive in small numbers in isolated places throughout the park. The Wonderland is one of those isolated places. Within the Wonderland, the sheep can find the rugged terrain, isolation, and water pockets that are essential for their survival.

The bighorn sheep that live in the park are very shy and nervous animals. Disturbances to their living patterns will cause them to become physically run-down; under stress, they cease to reproduce. For these reasons, the National Park Service has designated most of the Wonderland of Rocks as a day use area. This allows the sheep to roam undisturbed at

night and make their way to water sources. Although bighorn sheep are elusive, they are sometimes spotted on the rugged mountains and boulder formations. Occasionally in midsummer, they come down near the campground and park roads.

The nature trail can also be accessed from the group campground. The trail leaves the group campground at the camping limit sign between sites 11 and 12. This spur trail travels 1/8 mile and joins the main trail on the north side of the loop.

USGS Topographical Map: Indian Cove 7.5'   **Trail Map 4**

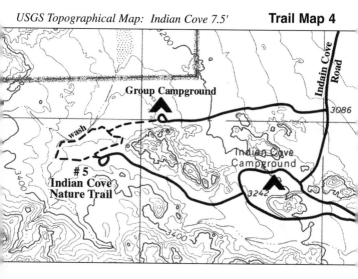

6   Boy Scout Trail

Highlights: variety of terrain, views, and vegetation; picturesque washes; steep narrow canyon; adjacent to Wonderland of Rocks

Mileage: 8 miles (one-way) **Time:** 4 -5 hours

Difficulty: moderate (downhill) **Map:** Trail Map 5

Elevation Difference: 1345' **Total Uphill Travel:** 219'

Use Restrictions: partial day use, no bicycles

Access: Wonderland Trailhead. Travel 2.3 miles west of Hidden Valley Campground or 6.4 miles east of the West Entrance Station on Park Boulevard. Park in the large parking lot on the north side of the road.

Finish: Indian Cove Trailhead, located on the west side of Indian Cove Road; 0.4 miles south of the Indian Cove Ranger Station

Elevation Profile

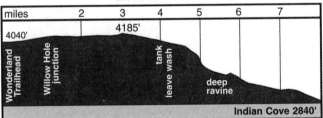

Description: The Boy Scout Trail provides a variety of terrain and views. The hike is described from south to north. From this direction, the trail travels mostly downhill to Indian Cove.

The first portion of the trail leads along the edge of the Wonderland of Rocks. It follows picturesque, sandy washes lined with junipers, pinyon pines, and oak trees. The latter portion of the trail travels along a rocky mountainside, winds through steep mountains and narrow canyons, then continues through the open desert to Indian Cove. There are many pleasant places for camping not far from the trail. Camping is only

allowed on the west side of the trail. The east side of the trail is day use only.

Follow the trail 1.4 miles north from the parking area to a fork. Take the trail to the left. (The right fork leads to a wash that descends into Willow Hole. For information on the Willow Hole route, refer to the book *On Foot in Joshua Tree National Park*.) About four miles from the parking lot, the trail makes a sharp left turn out of a wash. This turn may be poorly identified. Missing the turn will result in travel into a steep, nearly impassable canyon. To prevent this error, watch for a tank and water trough in the wash.

A tank is a barrier that spans the width of a wash. Pioneers used tanks during the ranching days to collect water for cattle. They built this particular tank by cementing small walls of rock on the sides of a natural boulder obstruction. The tank is filled with sand and no longer holds water.

About 300 yards beyond the tank and trough, the trail leaves the wash and heads west (left). The remainder of the trail should pose no problem. Note: This trail is also commonly hiked uphill from Indian Cove.

Hikers near the beginning of the Boy Scout Trail

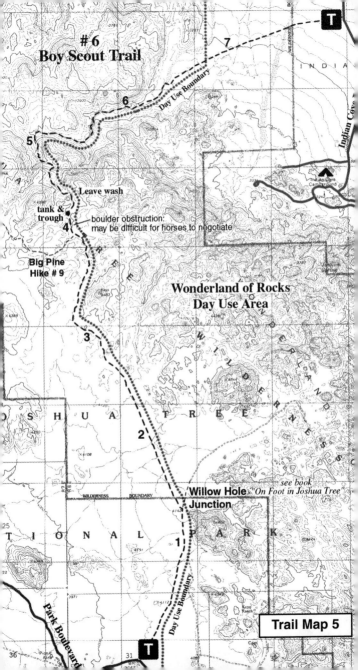

#6
Boy Scout Trail

7

INDIA

Day Use Boundary

6

5

Indian Cove

Campground

Leave wash

tank & trough

4

boulder obstruction: may be difficult for horses to negotiate

Big Pine Hike # 9

Wonderland of Rocks Day Use Area

W I L D E R N E S S

3

J O S H U A   T R E E

2

WILDERNESS BOUNDARY

see book **"On Foot in Joshua Tree"**

Willow Hole Junction

1

N A T I O N A L   P A R K

25

22

Keys Ranch

36

31

Park Boulevard

Day Use Boundary

Trail Map 5

7  **Fortynine Palms Oasis**

Highlights: beautiful isolated oasis in a rugged canyon
Mileage: 3 miles (round-trip)   **Time:** 2-3 hours
Difficulty: moderately strenuous   **Map:** Trail Map 6
Elevation Difference: 360'   **Total Uphill Travel:** 820'
Use Restrictions: day use only, no horses or bicycles
Access: Fortynine Palms Parking Area. Take Highway 62 to
Canyon Road in Twentynine Palms. Canyon Road is located 4
miles west of Adobe Road (traffic light) in 29 Palms or 1.75 miles
east of Indian Cove Road. Drive south to the end of Canyon Road.

Elevation Profile

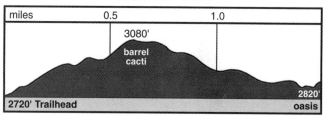

Description: Fortynine Palms is one of five oases in the park.
The life that revolves around all five of these vibrant green
oases contrasts with the arid surroundings in which they are
found. Water, either on the surface or not far below, nourish-
es concentrations of lush grasses, native fan palms, cottonwoods, and other water-loving plants.

The oases provide an important life source and home for
many species of plants, birds, and other wildlife. Fortynine
Palms Oasis, as well as the other oases in the park, is designated as a day use area because of its importance to bighorn sheep.
(See hike #5 for more information about desert bighorn sheep.)

USGS Topographical Map: Indian Cove 7.5'

The oasis is located in a rocky canyon. Over fifty native fan palms tower above clear pools of water lined with emerald-green algae. Under the oasis canopy, there are large polished boulders that provide a place to rest and enjoy the natural life and sounds of this miniature ecosystem.

The palm trees at Fortynine Palms Oasis look noticeably different from the trees at other oases. Many of the tree trunks are black. Larger trees are missing the characteristic skirts of dead palm fronds. This is the result of four fires that have swept through the area since 1940.

Oasis fires can be beneficial to palm trees. Fires kill the mesquite that competes for water and keeps sunlight from reaching palm seedlings. Recently burned palm trees usually produce more seeds, and hence more seedlings, than those trees that haven't burned.

The black palm trunks supporting a bright green canopy give this oasis a unique beauty. Some thoughtless hikers have carved into palm trunks. This distracts from the natural beauty of the area. Please don't add to the graffiti. Hopefully, the scarring will diminish with time.

The trail to the Fortynine Palms Oasis ascends to a ridge above the parking lot. Look for a concentrated display of barrel cacti on top of the ridge. The thick red spines and the large round shape of the plant itself make this cactus easy to identify. After winding around the ridgetop, the trail steeply descends the other side of the ridge to the oasis. The 1.5-mile trail ends at the oasis. Return to the parking lot over the same trail.

This trail was chosen as a "kid pick" because of the variety of sights that interest children—water, greenery, cacti, boulders, and palm trees. Due to the distance and elevation gain, the children should be fairly good hikers.

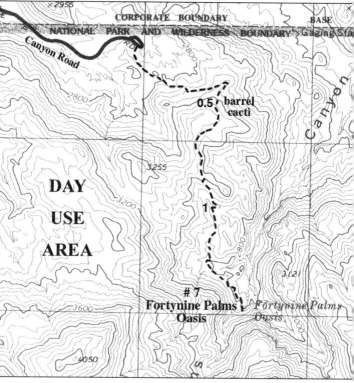

USGS Topographical Map: Queen Mtn. 7.5'   **Trail Map 6**

USGS Topographical Map: Twentynine Palms 7.5'   **Trail Map 7**

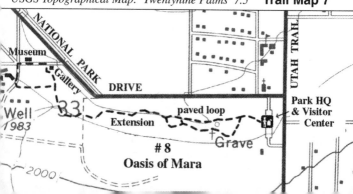

8   Oasis of Mara Twentynine Palms Oasis

Highlights: interpretive trail, oasis, historical site, bird life
Mileage: 0.5 mile loop (2 mile loop)   **Time:** < 1 hour, (1 hour)
Difficulty: easy   **Map:** Trail Map 7
Elevation Difference: relatively level
Use Restrictions: day use only, no horses or bicycles
Access: Oasis Visitor Center, corner of Utah Trail and National Park Drive in Twentynine Palms

---

Description: The Oasis of Mara has been a center of life throughout the history of man's presence in the Southern California Desert. Two tribes of Native Americans, the Serrano and the Chemehuevi, initially inhabited the oasis. Later prospectors and homesteaders moved into the area. When the white man arrived, this oasis provided a place of peaceful coexistence for both Native Americans and pioneers. Today the only reminder of man's historical presence at the oasis is the gravestone of a young woman who died in 1903. All dwellings and other signs of human habitation have long since vanished.

A paved loop trail circles beneath the rustling palms. Signs along the trail interpret the plants and animals of this miniature ecosystem and the history of the area. A few signs explain oasis management and prescribed burns. To improve biological diversity, the National Park Service periodically conducts controlled burns of this oasis. (See hike #7 for more on oasis fires.)

A dirt trail, known as the Oasis Trail Extension (1.5 mile loop), leaves from the back side of the paved loop and leads to the Twentynine Palms Art Gallery, Historical Society Museum, and the Twentynine Palms Inn. Numbered posts along the trail point out different plants and area highlights. Ask for the accompanying handout at the visitor center.

Chapter 3
Hikes Near Lost Horse Valley Campgrounds

Hidden Valley, Ryan, and Sheep Pass campgrounds are located in Lost Horse Valley. This beautiful Joshua tree forested valley is the busiest and most popular area in the park. It is surrounded by some of the park's tallest mountains. Just north of the valley lies the Wonderland of Rocks—an incredible jumbled maze of massive monzogranite boulder piles that extends over twelve square miles. (See hike #18 for geologic details on the boulder formations.) These unique boulder piles attract climbers, hikers, and sightseers from around the world.

Hidden Valley Campground has 39 sites nestled in the nooks of the Wonderland boulder formations. The 31 sites at Ryan Campground circle an isolated grouping of boulders on the southeast edge of the valley. Ryan has a separate horse site. Both campgrounds are free and are available on a first-come-first-served basis.

Sheep Pass Campground sits at the base of Ryan Mountain on a low pass separating Lost Horse and Queen valleys. It has six group sites and no individual sites. There is a fee and reservations are required.

There are tables, fire grates, and vault toilets at all three campgrounds. There is no water. Water is available at the West Entrance Station (14 miles away) or at the Oasis Visitor Center in Twentynine Palms (about 20 miles away). The nearest towns with shopping facilities are Twentynine Palms and Yucca Valley, both about 20 miles from Hidden Valley Campground.

To reach Lost Horse Valley, take Highway 62 to the town of Joshua Tree. Turn south on Park Boulevard and drive about 14 miles. If you are coming from the east, enter the park through the North Entrance and follow Park Boulevard about 13 miles.

For additional hikes from this area, see Chapter 2, hike #6 and Chapter 6, hikes #34 and #35.

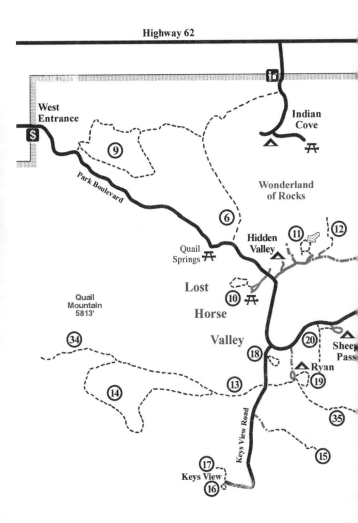

9 [10] △ 🏇 North View / Maze / Window Rock Loop

Highlights: variety of terrain, views and vegetation; thunderbird-shaped rock window; high vistas; boulder maze

Mileage: 6.6 mile loop
Time: 4-6 hours

Difficulty: moderately strenuous
Map: Trail Map 8

Elevation Difference: 390'
Total Uphill Travel: 835'

Use Restrictions: no bicycles

Access: Borrow Pit Parking Area. From the West Entrance, drive 1.8 miles east on Park Boulevard. There is a small parking area on a bend on the north (left) side of the road. Note: A large parking lot, in the same general location, is forthcoming for this trailhead.

Elevation Profile

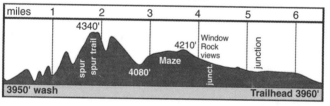

Description: This newly designated trail has much to offer. It leads to high vistas and travels past an odd shaped window located high up on a rocky hill. The trail covers varied terrain including rolling hills, steep mountainsides, high ridgetops, sheltered ravines, wide desert washes, and gentle open areas. For a short section, the trail winds through an area of boulders known as the Maze.

Vegetation is equally varied with large nolinas, yuccas, junipers, pines, cacti, and of course, Joshua trees. Under the right spring conditions, beautiful blue Canterberry bell flowers are abundant.

From the parking lot, walk up a dirt roadway about 40 yards. Head left on the trail that crosses the road. Travel 75

yards and take a sharp right at a fork in the trail. Follow the trail to the northeast side of a gravel pit then into a wash. As the gravel pit disappears behind a low ridge, the trail forks again. Take the left fork. The trail that continues straight up the wash is the Maze Loop cutoff (see options below). Note: When the new parking lot is created at the trailhead, the trail start will change. New signs should prevent confusion.

From this junction, the trail begins winding up through rolling rocky hills that sit between larger boulder-covered mountains. The trail climbs repeatedly up and down from ridgetops to ravines.

At mile 1.6, a short spur trail (0.2 miles) leads to a precipice boasting broad views of the desert towns and mountains located north of the park. About 1/4 mile farther along the main trail, a shorter spur leads to another ridgetop view. From here, there are excellent views of the park interior—over to Park Boulevard and beyond to Quail Mountain, the highest mountain in the park. (Look below for the miniaturized cars at the trailhead to gain an increased sense of accomplishment for your ascent efforts.)

From the second spur, the trail follows a ridge and begins a gradual descent into a drainage. A final short steep section brings the trail into a small wash. Travel down this wash a short distance to intersect a larger wash. Turn right, go sixty yards, then take the left fork. Follow the trail markers through this potentially confusing area of washes and drainages. The trail will become more visible shortly.

At mile 3, there is another trail junction. The left fork is the Big Pine Trail; it leads over to the Boy Scout Trail (see options below). Take the southern trail (right fork) to continue the loop. Within 1/4 mile, the trail passes the Maze Loop cutoff. Continue to the left at this fork.

The trail soon enters the Maze at the base of a large boulder-covered mountain. Wind through the narrow passages that lead through piles of low boulder mounds. In this section, there are several beautiful large nolina plants near the trail.

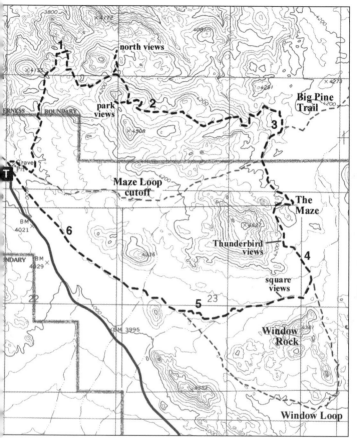

USGS Topographical Map: Indian Cove 7.5'   **Trail Map 8**

As the trail leaves the Maze and heads out into the open, Window Rock becomes visible. These early views of Window Rock are the most striking. On top of the most prominent rocky peak to the south appears an opening in the shape of a thunderbird (an upright side profile of a bird with its huge wings outstretched). Later, as the trail continues past the front of this peak, the window transforms into an ordinary square.

At mile 4.3, the trail enters a wash. (Continuing across the wash leads to a southern loop trail around Window Rock—see options below.) At this junction, turn right (west) and head down the wash in front of Window Rock. In about 1/2 mile, the trail exits the wash and begins a gradual turn back to the north. At mile 5.2, the trail passes the second junction with the southern loop. Head northwest (right). From here back to the parking area, the trail travels over fairly level terrain forested with Joshua trees.

Hike Options

Maze Loop: This trail bypasses the rocky hills to the north. It shortens the loop by 1.6 miles; however, it misses much of the interesting terrain and views for which this hike is noted.

Big Pine Trail: This 1.8 mile trail leads to the mid point of the Boy Scout Trail (see hike #6). A 0.6 mile spur leads north from the Big Pine Trail to a large pine tree with a diameter of about 3'. This lone pine is unusually large for a desert pine. Other natural features that deserve mentioning are large groups of barrel cacti and a quartz outcropping. The barrel cacti border the trail about one mile from the North View/Big Pine trail junction. About 1/2 mile farther, the trail travels over a hill paved with large chunks of white quartz.

Window Loop: Taking this southern trail extension adds one mile to the hike. The trail leads around the base of the Window Rock peak through pleasant terrain and vegetation. The views of Window Rock are limited on this section.

10 🔟 🚶 🚶

Hidden Valley Nature Trail

Highlights: interpretive trail, valley surrounded by large boulder formations, popular rock climbing area
Mileage: 1 mile loop   **Time:** 1 hour
Difficulty: easy   **Map:** Trail Map 9
Elevation Difference: relatively level with rustic rock steps
Use Restrictions: day use only, no horses or bicycles
Access: Hidden Valley Picnic Area, on the south side of Park Boulevard, 14 miles east of the West Entrance Station

---

Description: Legend suggests that this rock-enclosed valley was a hideout for cattle and horse rustlers in the late 1800's. Rocky walls and massive boulder piles create a natural corral that could have contained the stolen cattle and horses.

Today, a narrow gap in the rocks provides the only easy entrance into the valley. Bill Keys, one of the early desert pioneers, created this gap in 1936. Keys blasted the opening into the valley to improve access for his legitimate cattle operation. (To learn more about the interesting life of Bill Keys, ask a park ranger about Desert Queen Ranch Tours.)

The Hidden Valley Nature Trail leaves the parking lot, passes through the narrow gap, and circles the perimeter of the valley. Joshua trees, those tall, spiny trees that are characteristic of the Mojave Desert, are scattered throughout the valley. Large oaks and pines grow in the shade of the valley's rocky walls. Signs along the trail discuss these plants and interpret other plants and animals supported by the valley's microclimate. Additionally, some signs discuss plant uses by early desert Indians, while others touch on recent human impacts to the area.

Hidden Valley is a popular area for sport climbing. Look for rock climbers on the many rock formations around the perimeter and in the middle of the valley. While scanning the

rocks for climbers, keep an eye out for the rock formation
known as the Trojan. This unusual face profile is near the
northeast corner of the loop.

This hike is enjoyable for children. They will particularly
like exploring around the many boulder piles and watching the
rock climbers. (Note: Parents keep a close eye on children lest
they scramble up too high on potentially dangerous rock piles.)

Trail Map 9   *USGS Topographical Map: Indian Cove 7.5'*

The Trojan

11 🔟 🚶 🚶 Barker Dam Nature Trail

Highlights: interpretive trail, historical site, small lake with water-loving plants and birds, petroglyphs, large boulder formations, rock climbing area

Mileage: 1.4 mile loop   **Time:** 1 hour

Difficulty: easy   **Map:** Trail Map 10

Elevation Difference: relatively level with rustic rock steps

Use Restrictions: day use only, no horses or bicycles

Access: Barker Dam Parking Area. Follow the road that leads northeast past the entrance to Hidden Valley Campground. Turn right at the "T" intersection. Take the next road leading to the left. Follow it to a large parking lot.

Description: Hiking through the Wonderland of Rocks is usually difficult. However, a few sandy washes that cut into the outer edge of the Wonderland provide easy hiking. Barker Dam is in one of these easily accessible areas.

Early cowboys originally built Barker Dam to collect water for cattle. Later, pioneer Bill Keys added six vertical feet to the dam. Keys renamed it "Bighorn Dam" and etched this new name into the top of the retaining wall. Today the dam holds a small, beautiful lake framed by the rugged boulders of the Wonderland.

The trail leads to the lake and dam. It loops around Piano Valley then returns to the parking lot. Signs along the way cover two themes. Near the lake, the signs interpret the plant and bird life surrounding a desert water source and discuss historical uses of the water by early Indians and pioneers. Along other sections of the trail, the signs interpret the plants and animals of the Mojave Desert and explain their adaptations for a dry environment.

Follow the trail 1/2 mile from the parking lot to the lake. This first section of trial leads through a narrow corridor bor-

dered by rocky walls and large oaks and pines. The trail leads west (left) along the lake's edge to the top of the dam. Water levels in the lake are dependent on the annual rainfall and the time of the year.

Follow the trail to the bottom of the dam. Take some time to examine the unusual watering trough below the dam. Bill Keys designed the trough to conserve water, a precious desert resource. The center ring of the trough protected a float device that prevented the trough from overflowing.

From the dam, follow the trail through the rock-enclosed Piano Valley. Notice the large boulder to the right of the trail at about mile 0.75. This rock is appropriately named Piano Rock. With imagination, it looks like a huge grand piano; however, it was named for another reason. In the late 1930's, locals organized musical camping trips to this area. According to Willis Keys, then a young local resident, a piano was placed on top of this boulder. The campers would then sit on Joshua tree logs and listen to a concert. Note the weathered gray logs still lined up at the base of the rock.

Travel about 150 yards past Piano Rock to a trail junction. Continue 100 feet beyond this junction to view some petroglyphs located in an elevated rock overhang. Petroglyphs are carvings made on the rocks by early Native Americans. Experts who study petroglyphs are still uncertain whether the carvings were a form of writing or just doodling. A film crew unfortunately painted over some of these petroglyphs in an attempt to make the carvings more visible. A few of the carvings located on the base of the overhang remain undamaged.

Backtrack to the trail junction and turn right (east). Follow the trail back to the parking lot.

12 🔟 🚶 Wonderland Ranch Wash

Highlights: picturesque wash, historical site, large boulder formations including gigantic boulder domes, rock climbing area
Mileage: 2 miles (round-trip)   **Time:** 1.5 hours
Difficulty: easy, with easy scrambling   **Map:** Trail Map 10
Elevation Difference: relatively level
Use Restrictions: day use only, no horses or bicycles
Access: Wonderland Ranch Parking Area. Follow the road that leads northeast past the entrance to Hidden Valley Campground. Turn right at the "T" intersection. Travel one mile. Take the second left; follow the short road to the end.

Description: Rock climbers frequently use this popular route to travel to the Astro Domes. The Astro Domes are a collection of giant, steep-faced boulders that provide climbers with some of the highest, most extreme climbs in the park. Some of these boulders tower over 300' above the wash. This hike provides an opportunity both to view some of these climbing extremists and to enjoy the natural beauty of the area.

This is not a well-defined trail, but merely a beaten path created by foot traffic. From the parking area, follow an old roadbed about 100 yards to a fork. Take the left fork and continue a short distance to the ruins of a pink house (former Wonderland Ranch). Head left (west) from the corner of the house and enter a wash fifty feet away. Travel northwest up the wash.

Watch for a thick growth of bushes and trees about 25 yards up the wash on the left side. Hidden behind the greenery is a site used first by early Indians and later by pioneers. Look under an overhanging boulder to find a cold storage compartment built by pioneers. On the nearby ledge, look for a bedrock mortar. A mortar is a smooth, deep hole in the rock

in which early Native Americans ground seeds, acorns, or other raw foods.

Follow the wash and the intermittent parallel trail as they wind around bushes, oak trees, cacti, and boulders in the rocky corridor. The wash emerges in the valley below the Astro Domes. Binoculars may be handy for viewing climbers high up on the rocky faces of the Domes. Return to the parking lot over the same route.

Trail Map 10   *USGS Topographical Map: Indian Cove 7.5'*

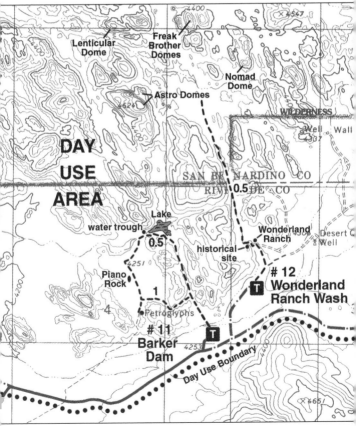

13 🔺🐎   Juniper Flats

Highlights: scenic vistas, large junipers, scenic wilderness camping, opportunity to see interesting effects of 1999 wildfires

Mileage: 9 miles (round-trip)   **Time:** 4 - 6 hours

Difficulty: moderate   **Map:** Trail Map 11

Elevation Difference: 431'   **Total Uphill Travel:** 634'

Use Restrictions: no bicycles

Access: Juniper Flats Trailhead, located on the right (west) side of Keys View Road; one mile south of Park Boulevard

Elevation Profile

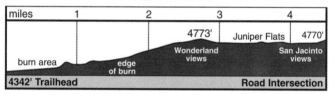

Description: Juniper Flats is an extensive, relatively level area thickly vegetated with large juniper trees. Quail Mountain (5813'), the highest mountain in the park, borders the area to the north. Mt. San Jacinto, a 10,804' peak located outside the park, can be seen to the southeast.

The great views and thick vegetation make Juniper Flats a scenic spot for backcountry camping. (Note the day use area boundaries on the map.) Juniper Flats is a favorite area for the mule deer that inhabit the park. Watch for signs of deer and other wildlife throughout the hike.

The first part of the trail travels through rolling hills along the boundary of a wildfire burn. In the summer of 1999, Joshua Tree National Park experienced the largest wildfires in its recorded history. Before the fires were out, almost 14,000 acres had burned. The effects of the fire appeared devastating

to those who viewed the massive fire-blackened areas that year. However, less than two years later, many of the burned areas were vibrant with life. The Juniper Flats trail travels through one of these areas. The trail begins by traveling through an area of fire spotting—live Joshua trees grow side by side with burnt trees. Farther on, the trail travels through more solid burn areas.

The trail climbs a knoll 0.8 miles from the trailhead. Look back from the knoll and notice the striking difference between the burned and unburned areas. The unburned hillside is thick with smoky-green black brush. In the burnt area below, the heavy brush is gone; it's replaced by a vibrant green carpet of annual plants (depending upon rain levels and the time of year).

Note that the Joshua trees and yucca plants are making a comeback. Joshua trees are not fire resistant; with their shaggy bark, they ignite like fire sticks. Once burned, they cannot recover. However, they can reproduce by sending new shoots up from underground runners. Notice the many Joshua tree sprouts, already over a foot high, growing beneath the fire-killed trees.

Around mile 2, the trail leaves the burn area and begins to travel through large junipers. Halfway to the flats, the trail follows a ridge offering excellent views of the Wonderland.

The trail intersects a dirt road (closed to vehicles) 4.5 miles from the trailhead. This intersection marks the end of the described hike. The road continues north another 1/2 mile to the base of Quail Mountain. Continuing on the trail will lead to Covington Flats (see hike #34).

Joshua trees frame Mt. San Jacinto at Juniper Flats.

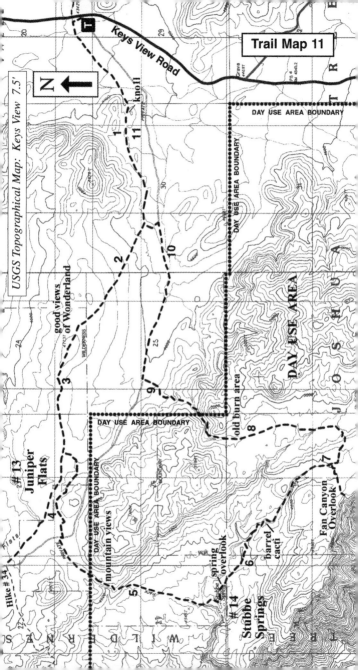

Trail Map 11

USGS Topographical Map: Keys View 7.5'

N

Keys View Road

knoll

DAY USE AREA BOUNDARY

DAY USE AREA BOUNDARY

good views
of Wonderland

WILDERNESS

DAY USE AREA BOUNDARY

old burn area

DAY USE AREA

JOSHUA

DAY USE AREA BOUNDARY

#13
Juniper
Flats

mountain views

Hike #34

Fan Canyon
Overlook

barrel
cacti

spring overlook

#14
Stubbe
Springs

WILDERNESS

14 🔟 🔺 🐎 Stubbe Spring Loop

Highlights: beautiful quiet desert wilderness; scenic vistas; large vegetation; desert water source; interesting wildfire burn areas
Mileage: 12 mile loop　　　　**Time:** 6‑8 hours
Difficulty: moderately strenuous　　**Map:** Trail Map 11
Elevation Difference: 630'　　**Total Uphill Travel:** 1077'
Use Restrictions: partial day use, no bicycles
Access: Juniper Flats Trailhead, located on the right (west) side of Keys View Road; one mile south of Park Boulevard

Elevation Profile

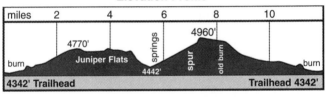

Description: In a nutshell, this newly designated trail offers a beautiful, quiet wilderness experience in the desert. The trail travels through a variety of terrain, vegetation, and views. It leads over mountains and ridgetops and through valleys, canyons, and washes. Highlights include a rare desert water source, a dramatic vista, fire burned areas, and areas of large thick vegetation. Given the remoteness, the only man-made sounds you will hear will be from an occasional distant jet.

The first part of the hike follows the Juniper Flats trail (see hike #13). At mile 1.6, there is a junction for Stubbe Spring Loop. Bypass this junction, and continue to a second junction at mile 3.5. Watch for a trail sign. The beginning of the Stubbe Springs Loop trail branches off the left side of the Juniper Flats trail. (This hike is easier and more pleasant when hiked counterclockwise around the loop.)

Follow the trail about 3/4 mile to intersect a dirt road. Turn right and travel 35 yards up the road to a fork. This fork is a good spot to take note of two areas with contrasting vegetation. The adjacent hills to the south have a thick covering of green pines and junipers. Now look north to Quail Mountain, which appears stark, brown and devoid of vegetation. Being the highest point in the park, Quail Mountain is susceptible to lightning strikes. Wildfires, including the 1999 fires, have burned this mountain many times over the years.

Turn left at the fork and continue to follow a road. The road soon disintegrates into an overgrown jeep trail. The trail travels along a hillside from where there are views of Mt. San Gorgonio (11,499'), Mt. San Jacinto (10,804'), and the distant Santa Rosa Mountains. A rocky descent leads to a sandy flat area. (The trail is prone to wash outs in this area so watch for trail markers or rock cairns.)

At mile 5.4, the trail enters a drainage and moves repeatedly in and out of washes for about 1/8 mile. Watch the sides of the drainages to keep track of the trail. The trail will soon climb steeply out of the wash on the left (south) side. Follow the trail up the ridge and make a sharp left turn. At this point, the trail becomes much easier to follow.

Within a short distance, Stubbe Spring comes into view on the right side of the trail. Despite the absence of surface water at the spring, there is a thick tangle of greenery. Tall grasses, sedges, and willows carpet the hillside and the drainage below the spring. Because Stubbe Spring is an important site for wildlife, the National Park Service has designated it for day use only. (See hike #5 to understand the important link between day use areas and bighorn sheep.)

The trail follows a ridge about a half-mile then descends into a wash. Turn right and travel up the wash about one mile to a signed junction at mile 7. A spur trail departs the wash on the right and leads to a must-see vista. The 1/4-mile spur ends at the edge of a dramatic precipice. Beyond the viewpoint, the ground drops steeply away revealing Fan Canyon, 2000'

directly below. Look out past the canyon for views of the low desert cities and distant mountain ranges.

From the spur junction, continue in the wash a short distance. The trail leaves the left side of the wash and begins a climb to a plateau. Follow the trail across the plateau to reach an old burn area. Black juniper and pine tree skeletons still stand, but the Joshua trees are blown over and weathered gray. Compare this stark landscape to the pine-covered canyon a few hundred yards farther down the trail.

The trail winds down the canyon then heads out into the open area near Juniper Flats. At this point, Joshua trees become the prominent vegetation; the trail passes by several large trees.

At mile 9, the trail intersects a dirt road. Follow the road down to the right about one mile. While traveling the road, note that the road was a fire line for the 1999 wildfires. There are burnt trees to the left and an unmarred landscape to the right.

Look for a sign signifying the departure of the trail from the road. Follow the trail a short distance back to the Juniper Flats trail. Turn right and continue the remaining 1.6 miles back to the parking lot. (Note: It is possible to follow the dirt road back to the parking lot. However, the road is sandy, which makes walking difficult.)

Lost Horse Mine Stamp Mill

15 🔼🐴   Lost Horse Mine

Highlights: historical mine site, good vistas
Mileage: 4 miles (round-trip)   **Time:** 2-3 hours
Difficulty: moderate   **Map:** Trail Map 12
Elevation Difference: 480'   **Total Uphill Travel:** 738'
Use Restrictions: partial day use, no bicycles
Access: Lost Horse Mine Parking Area. Follow Keys View Road
south 2.4 miles from Park Boulevard. Turn left (east) onto a dirt
road and follow it to the end.

Elevation Profile

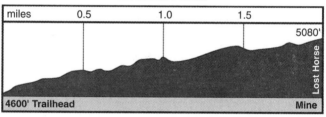

Description: The Lost Horse Mine operation was one of the
most successful gold mining operations within the park.
Frank Diebold, a German prospector, initially discovered the
gold strike. However, it was Johnny Lang who was responsi-
ble for making the mine productive.

As the story goes, Lang was looking for a lost horse in
1893 when he came across Diebold's mining camp. Shortly
thereafter, Diebold sold his discovery rights to Johnny Lang
and his father. Johnny and his new partners, Thomas and Jep
Ryan (see hike #19), started up the Lost Horse Mine operation
around 1895. Over the next ten years, they processed several
thousand ounces of gold.

The existing structures of this mine are among the best
preserved mining structures within the National Park System.

Although many of the buildings have been leveled, the significant remains of the ten-stamp mill are still standing. Several large cyanide settling tanks, stone building foundations, and miscellaneous mining equipment surround the mill. Most of the mine shafts have been fenced or sealed. (Mine shafts are dangerous; maintain a safe distance from their openings.)

The trail, once a wagon road, gradually winds up through rolling hills to the mine. Note the lack of Joshua trees and pinyon pines around the mine area. The trees were used for fuel during the mining days and have yet to regenerate.

Take the additional short, steep hike (NE) to the top of the hill (5188') behind the stamp mill. The hilltop offers good views of Pleasant Valley, Pinto Basin, Mt. San Gorgonio, Mt. San Jacinto, Lost Horse Valley, and the Wonderland of Rocks.

Trail Map 12   *USGS Topographical Map: Keys View 7.5'*

16 🚶 Keys View Loop

Highlights: spectacular views, interpretive signs
Mileage: 0.25 mile loop   **Time:** < 1 hour
Difficulty: easy   **Map:** Trail Map 13
Elevation Difference: 40'
Use Restrictions: day use only, no horses or bicycles
Access: Keys View Parking Area, end of Keys View Road

Description: Keys View sits on the crest of the Little San Bernardino Mountains. It is the highest point in the park reached by paved road. The area is well known for its spectacular view of the Coachella Valley, Mt. San Jacinto, Mt. San Gorgonio, and the Salton Sea. A short paved trail ascends steeply to a high viewpoint of these landmarks and several other points of interest—the Santa Rosa Mountains, Indio, Palm Springs, the San Andreas Fault, and Signal Mountain in Mexico (90 miles to the south). There are viewing benches and large interpretive signs spaced along the trail.

The panorama is outstanding; however, a haze frequently diminishes the view. The pollution, which rolls in from the Los Angeles metropolis, has become increasingly more evident over the past several years. It has become so evident that the National Park Service has installed a sign addressing differing smog levels. Generally there will be less smog on calmer, cooler days. Additionally, visibility is usually better after a hard rain.

17 [10] Inspiration Peak (5558')

> **Highlights:** spectacular views, peak climb
> **Mileage:** 1.4 miles (round-trip)   **Time:** 1.5 hours
> **Difficulty:** moderately strenuous   **Map:** Trail Map 13
> **Elevation Difference:** 408'   **Total Uphill Travel:** 604'
> **Use Restrictions:** day use only, no horses or bicycles
> **Access:** Keys View Parking Area, end of Keys View Road

Elevation Profile

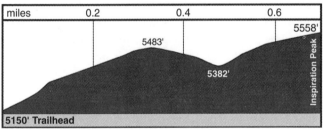

Description: Inspiration Peak lies a short distance from Keys View on the crest of the Little San Bernardino Mountains. The panoramic view from Inspiration Peak is even more impressive and more encompassing than the view from Keys View Loop (see hike #16). The circular vista includes a more extensive view of the Coachella Valley and the Salton Sea, as well as splendid views of the park interior—the Wonderland, Queen and Lost Horse valleys, and part of the Pinto Basin.

Begin at the northwest side of the parking lot. (There may be a small trail marker at the trailhead.) The trail travels up to and along a broad high point, descends to a saddle, then continues up to the actual summit. There are good views from the first high point. However, the best views are obtained from the summit of the impressive, steep-faced peak at the end of

the trail. The last 50' of the trail may be difficult to follow. If you lose the trail, just scramble the remaining distance up the rock pile to the summit.

USGS Topographical Map: Keys View 7.5'   **Trail Map 13**

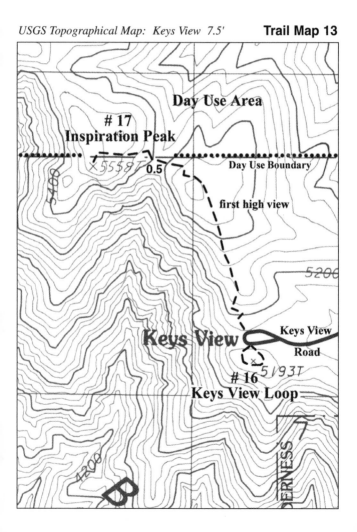

18 🚸🚶♿ Cap Rock Nature Trail

Highlights: interpretive trail, large boulder formations, popular rock climbing area

Mileage: 0.4 mile loop   **Time:** < 1 hour

Difficulty: easy   **Map:** Trail Map 14

Elevation Difference: relatively level

Use Restrictions: day use only, no horses or bicycles

Access: Cap Rock Parking Area, the first parking area on the left (east) side of Keys View Road; 0.2 miles from Park Boulevard

Description: The unique collection of gigantic boulder piles is a natural curiosity found in the park. The Cap Rock formation is one of these unusual piles of stone. The mere sight of this geologic oddity makes one wonder what magnificent force rolled the rocks together to create the formations.

The boulder piles were actually formed underground. Liquid rock oozed up, cooled, and crystallized beneath the core of existing older rock known as Pinto Gneiss. This younger, igneous rock, called monzogranite, formed with many irregularly spaced horizontal and vertical joints or cracks. Water filtered down through the Pinto Gneiss into the joints of the monzogranite. The water caused a chemical reaction that transformed the outer layers of this new rock into clay.

Uplifting and erosion of the Pinto Gneiss gradually worked to expose the monzogranite rock to the earth's surface. Once exposed, the soft clay covering the monzogranite eroded away leaving the rocks with rounded edges. As the clay eroded from the joints, the large rocks collapsed into piles creating the boulder formations.

A large rock perched like a visor on top of a massive pile of boulders prompted the naming of the Cap Rock formation. A level, paved trail leaves Cap Rock and circles through

smaller boulder formations. Signs along the trail identify the plants and discuss relationships between the plants and Mojave Desert wildlife. Some signs explain plant adaptations for surviving in a desert environment. Around the halfway point, there is a bench that sits in the shade of a large overhanging boulder. It's a good spot to sit and enjoy nature.

Cap Rock is a popular climbing area. Watch for climbers on the Cap Rock formation as well as on the smaller formations in the area. Children will enjoy doing their own exploring and scrambling over low boulder piles along the trail. (Note: Keep a close eye on children, lest they scramble up too high on potentially dangerous rock piles.)

USGS Topographical Map: Keys View 7.5'   **Trail Map 14**

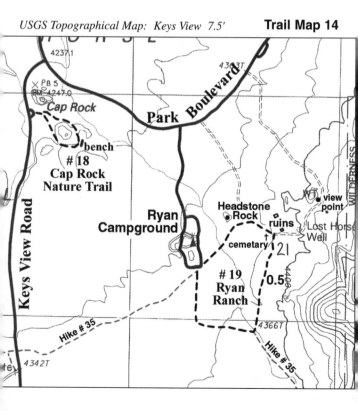

19 🚶🏇 Ryan Ranch Homestead

Highlights: historical adobe ranch ruins, good views, headstone rock formation

Mileage: 1 mile loop   **Time:** 1 hour

Difficulty: easy   **Map:** Trail Map 14

Elevation Difference: relatively level

Use Restrictions: day use only, no bicycles

Access: Ryan Campground Trailhead. Drive through the campground to reach a small parking lot on the southeast corner of the loop road. The trail starts near the restroom.

Description: Not far from Ryan Campground, lie the remains of an old ranch. This homestead belonged to the Ryan brothers, Jep and Thomas, two of the Lost Horse Mine owners (see hike #15). The brothers established the homestead to gain a reliable water source for their mining operations.

The most interesting remains at the homestead are the red adobe ruins. The largest ruin was a three-room ranch house built around 1900. It burnt in 1978, but the outer walls still stand. Look out the window openings and enjoy the view from the house. It is no wonder the Ryans picked this site for the house.

Near the ranch, there is an old cemetery with about eight graves. Rings of rocks, which have become hidden by vegetation, are the only markers for most of the grave sites. A couple of the graves have dates, ranging from 1893–1897, painted on nearby boulders. Judging from the size of the rock circles, at least one of the graves might have belonged to an infant.

For easier trail finding, clockwise travel is recommended. The trail travels trough Joshua trees and small boulder piles as it leads a short distance to the edge of Headstone Rock. This large overhanging boulder block provides a dramatic route for rock climbers.

At mile 0.2, the trail intersects the old road that leads to the ranch house. Turn right and follow the road 0.1 miles. There are two boulder piles along the right side of the road. Look for the cemetery near the smaller of the two piles.

Just past the cemetery, there is a cultural site sign. At this point, the driveway to the ranch house departs the left side of the road. Just beyond the sign, the loop trail leaves the right side of the road and follows a remnant jeep trail.

As a side trip, it is worth following the road an extra 1/4 mile. The road leads past another small adobe ruin, the remains of a windmill, and a well house. It continues uphill to a good viewpoint located on the south side of a large boulder cluster.

The loop trail continues south from the homestead to intersect the California Riding and Hiking Trail. Turn right at this junction and follow the trail back to the parking lot.

Climber on Headstone Rock

20 Ryan Mountain (5457')

> **Highlights:** great panoramic views of the park, peak climb
> **Mileage:** 3 miles (round-trip)   **Time:** 2-3 hours
> **Difficulty:** moderately strenuous   **Map:** Trail Map 15
> **Elevation Difference:** 1067'   **Total Uphill Travel:** 1067'
> **Use Restrictions:** no horses or bicycles
> **Access:** Ryan Mountain Parking Area, west of Sheep Pass

Elevation Profile

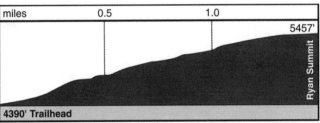

Description: The Ryan Mountain trail and summit provide some of the best panoramic views in the park. The 360° view from the summit includes Mt. San Jacinto, Mt. San Gorgonio, most of the park valleys, Pinto Basin, the Wonderland of Rocks, and more. The trail travels continuously uphill. There are several sections of stone steps constructed from rocks found in the area.

While traveling up the trail, look west to the rock formation known as Saddle Rocks. Watch for rock climbers. The longest technical climbing routes in the park are on this formation.

The Ryan Mountain trail can also be accessed from Sheep Pass Campground. A spur trail leaves from both site #1 and across the campground road from site #6. Hiking from Sheep Pass adds 1.5 miles round-trip. This spur trail joins the main trail about 0.2 miles from the Ryan Mountain Parking Area.

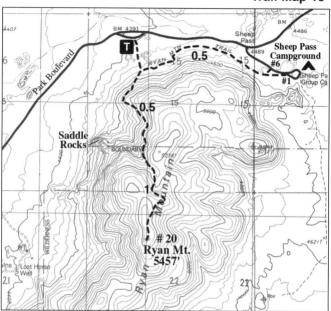

USGS Topographical Maps: Keys View, Indian Cove 7.5'

*The view from Ryan Mountain includes
Mt. San Jacinto towering above Lost Horse Valley.*

Chapter 4
Hikes Near Queen Valley
Campgrounds

Jumbo Rocks, Belle, and White Tank campgrounds are located on the eastern side of Queen Valley. This valley contains one of the larger Joshua tree forests in the park. Mountains bound the valley—Ryan Mountain to the west, Queen Mountain to the north, the Pinto Mountains to the east, and the Hexie Mountains to the south.

In the east half of the valley, there is a grouping of boulder piles similar to the Wonderland of Rocks but on a smaller scale. The 125 sites at Jumbo Rocks Campground are in the midst of this boulder group. Two smaller campgrounds, Belle with 18 sites and White Tank with 15 sites, are also located in boulder piles. These two boulder groups are separate from the large boulder maze near Jumbo Rocks.

All three campgrounds are free of charge and available on a first-come-first-served basis. Facilities include tables, fire grates, and vault toilets. There is no water. The nearest town with shopping facilities is Twentynine Palms, 10 to 11 miles north of the campgrounds. Water can be obtained at the Oasis Visitor Center, which is also located in Twentynine Palms.

To reach these campgrounds, take Highway 62 to the town of Twentynine Palms. Turn south on either National Park Drive or Utah Trail. Both roads lead past the Oasis Visitor Center and Park Headquarters. Continue south on Utah Trail through the North Entrance Station to the Pinto Wye road junction, 8 miles south of the visitor center.

From Pinto Wye, the Pinto Basin Road leads to the southern boundary of the park. Take this road to reach Belle and White Tank campgrounds, located about one and three miles south of the junction. Park Boulevard heads east through the

park to the West Entrance Station. Jumbo Rocks sits on the south side of Park Boulevard about three miles from Pinto Wye.

For additional hikes from this area, see Chapter 6, hikes #35, #36, and #37.

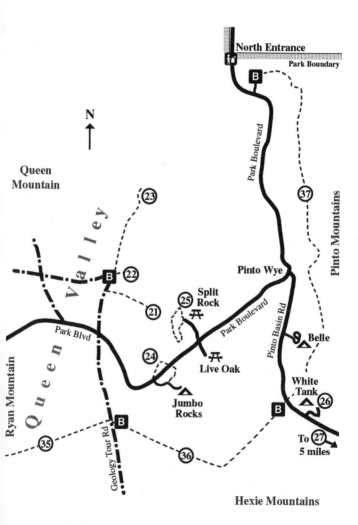

21 Lucky Boy Vista

Highlights: high viewpoint, overlook of Split Rock boulder maze

Mileage: 2.5 miles (round-trip)   **Time:** 2 hours

Difficulty: easy   **Map:** Trail Map 16

Elevation Difference: 100'   **Total Uphill Travel:** 204'

Use Restrictions: no bicycles

Access: Lucky Boy Junction. Follow the dirt road that leads north off Park Boulevard, opposite the Geology Tour Road. Travel about 0.8 miles to a parking spot on the right side of the road.

Elevation Profile

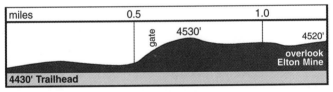

Description: This hike leads to a high, level plateau that provides both good views and some fine places to camp. The trail, an old mining road, travels through the eastern edge of Queen Valley. It winds through large boulders then climbs a short distance to reach a plateau. From the plateau, there are views of the rocky Eagle Cliff Hills and down into the rugged drainages that lead north to Desert Queen Mine.

The trail ends at an overlook above the Split Rock boulder maze. The Elton Mine, which consists of several vertical shafts, is at the end of the trail. The majority of the shafts are fenced; however, there are large holes in the fencing that children could slip through. (Mine shafts are dangerous; maintain a safe distance from their openings.)

From the parking lot, follow the trail east over relatively level ground. About halfway to the mine, the trail begins a

short but rapid ascent. Near the base of the ascent, there is a
gate barring the road. Travel around the gate and continue up
to the plateau. Follow the trail across the plateau to reach the
overlook.

USGS Topographical Map: Queen Mtn. 7.5'   **Trail Map 16**

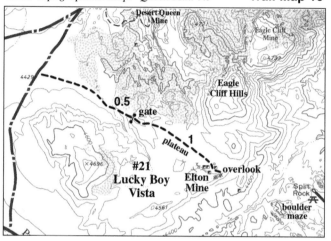

USGS Topographical Map: Queen Mtn. 7.5'   **Trail Map 17**

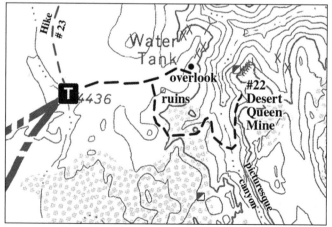

22 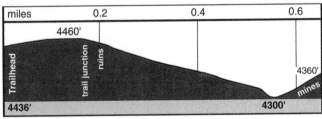 Desert Queen Mine

Highlights: historical ruins, mining equipment, picturesque ravine
Mileage: 1.5 miles (round-trip)   **Time:** 1.5 hours
Difficulty: moderate   **Map:** Trail Map 17
Elevation Difference: 160'   **Total Uphill Travel:** 244'
Use Restrictions: day use only, no horses or bicycles
Access: Pine City Backcountry Board. Follow the dirt road that leads north off Park Boulevard, opposite the Geology Tour Road. Park at the end of the road (1.2 miles).

Elevation Profile

| miles | 0.2 | 0.4 | 0.6 |

4460'
trail junction
ruins
Trailhead
4436'
4360'
mines
4300'

Description: The Desert Queen Mine was one of the most profitable and longest-operating (1895–1961) mines in the park area. According to the US Bureau of Mines, it produced 3,845 ounces of gold that, in turn, yielded several million dollars. Machinery, stone building ruins, and several mine shafts dot the hillsides in a concentrated area above the Desert Queen Wash. Today, steel grates block most of the shafts. Look through the grates to view the shaft structure, part of the rail system, and equipment used within the mines.

Follow the trail 300 yards from the east side of the parking lot to a junction. The main trail branches off and heads south (right). However, it is worth continuing straight an additional 0.1 miles to an overlook above the mine area. A sign at this overlook explains the history of the mine.

Backtrack to the trail junction and head south. The ruins of a stone building, used during the mining days, are located beside the trail near the junction. The trail continues past the ruins and travels south down to a sandy ravine. Cross the wash to find the trail leading up the other side of the ravine. The majority of the mine shafts are near the end of the trail.

While in the ravine, take some time to walk up the wash and explore the picturesque canyon. The wash winds below steep rocky walls as it travels through trees and giant boulders.

23 Pine City

Highlights: isolated area of desert greenery and boulders
Mileage: 3 miles (round-trip) **Time:** 2 hours
Difficulty: easy **Map:** Trail Map 18
Elevation Difference: 127' **Total Uphill Travel:** 141'
Use Restrictions: partial day use, partial bicycle route
Access: Pine City Backcountry Board. Follow the dirt road that leads north off Park Boulevard, opposite the Geology Tour Road. Park at the end of the road (1.2 miles).

Elevation Profile

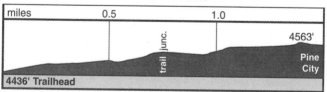

Description: It takes less than an hour to hike to Pine City, but it can take more than a day to explore and enjoy the quiet solitude of this pretty area. The area was not a city or town.

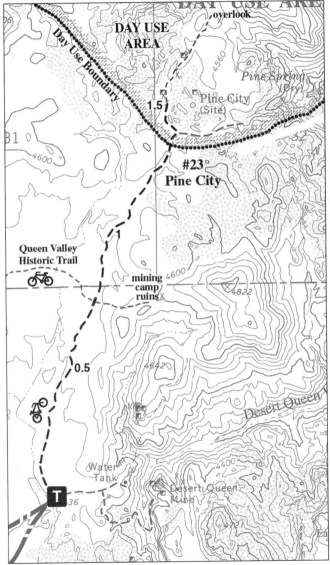

Trail Map 18   *USGS Topographical Map: Queen Mtn. 7.5'*

At most, there were one or two small cabins which are now gone. A few collapsed mine shafts are the only remains of this small mining area.

However, it is the island of desert greenery, and not the history, that draws hikers to this area. Large pine trees grow among an isolated collection of rocky walls and boulder mounds. This is an excellent place for bird watching. Bighorn sheep are known to inhabit the area, particularly in the summer months.

The trail heads north from the parking lot over gentle terrain. The first 3/4 mile of the trail is open to bicycle use. The trail is hard-packed, making biking easy. However, because of some sandy spots and sharp rocks, the trail is not recommended for children on bikes.

Hikers and bikers part company 3/4 of a mile from the parking lot. At this junction, the bike route makes a sharp left and continues over the Queen Valley Historic Road Trail. The bike route leads west about 4 miles, along the base of Queen Mountain, to the Wonderland Ranch Parking Area (see hike #12). It is definitely a hard-core mountain bike trail. The route is bushy, sandy, and in spots, difficult to follow.

At the same junction, another spur trail branches off to the right (east). This rocky overgrown spur leads to a ridge and the remains of a mining camp. Continue on the main trail to reach Pine City.

Upon reaching the Pine City boulder area, the trail travels to the west around the boulders and up to an overlook of a deep ravine. The mine shafts are along this section of the trail. (Mine shafts are dangerous; maintain a safe distance from their openings.)

Because Pine City is such an important area for wildlife, it is designated as a day use area. Camping is allowed in the more open areas just south of the Pine City boulders.

24 Skull Rock Nature Trail

Highlights: interpretive trail, Skull Rock formation, boulder piles

Mileage: 1.65 mile loop	**Time:** 1 hour
Difficulty: easy	**Map:** Trail Map 19
Elevation Difference: 120'	**Total Uphill Travel:** 166'

Use Restrictions: day use only, no horses or bicycles

Access: Jumbo Rocks Campground, just past the Loop E entrance

Elevation Profile

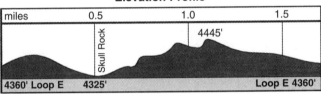

Description: This trail meanders through boulders, desert washes, and a rocky alleyway. Signs along the trail identify plants, explain the geology of the Mojave Desert, discuss plant and animal relationships, and describe plant uses by early Native Americans. The trail leads to Skull Rock, an unusual rock formation that can be viewed from the trail as well as from the road. The huge monzogranite boulder resembles a gigantic human skull. Large concave depressions form the skull's eye sockets and nostrils.

Access the trail from one of three locations: the entrance to Jumbo Rocks Campground; near the entrance to Loop E in the campground; or at Skull Rock, a pullout located a short distance east of the campground entrance. The recommended and described starting point is near Loop E.

The trail travels 1/2 mile from the campground to Skull Rock. The interpretive signs are located on this first portion of the trail. At Skull Rock, the trail crosses the road and con-

tinues on the other side. It travels through rocky alleys and climbs along a boulder slab as it leads to the campground entrance. The last 0.4 miles of the loop follow the campground road back to the trailhead near Loop E.

USGS Topographical Map: Malapai Hill 7.5'   **Trail Map 19**

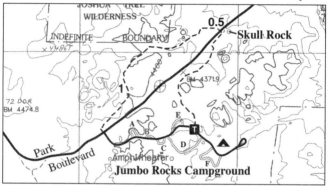

Skull Rock

25 Split Rock Loop

Highlights: face rock, tulip rock, boulder maze, dense yucca plants

Mileage: 2 mile loop   **Time:** 1 - 2 hours

Difficulty: easy   **Map:** Trail Map 20

Elevation Difference: 130'   **Total Uphill Travel:** 265'

Use Restrictions: day use only, no bicycles

Access: Split Rock Picnic Area, located on the north side of Park Boulevard, two miles west of the Pinto Wye road junction

---

Elevation Profile

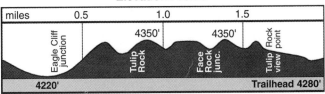

Description: Split Rock Loop is one of several newly designated park trails. It winds through a boulder maze and leads to some interesting rock formations. Traveling counterclockwise, the first part of the loop leads through thick stands of yucca plants as it weaves around isolated rock mounds. The latter part of the loop travels more deeply into the maze, through large steep-faced boulder piles.

The trail starts at Split Rock, a massive boulder that is split in two. From the parking lot, walk around the left side of Split Rock to a cave on the rock's north side. The cave is formed by the overhanging edges of the giant boulder. The trail heads north from the cave.

At 0.3 miles, there is a junction for the Eagle Cliff route. (For information on the Eagle Cliff route, refer to the book *On Foot in Joshua Tree National Park*.) Take a sharp left at this junction and follow the trail southwest.

Around mile 1.3, watch for a sign identifying a junction on the right (south) side of the trail. From this junction, a short side trip leads through a wash to Face Rock. This rock somewhat resembles the profile of President George Washington.

To reach Face Rock, travel down the wash about 300 yards from the junction. The wash leads past an old watering trough and continues to a rock wall where it becomes choked between the wall and a large juniper tree. The rock wall is Face Rock; however, the face is easier to see before reaching the wall. To continue on the loop trail, backtrack up the wash to the junction.

Another interesting rock formation is Tulip Rock. Look for this towering formation off the left (northwest) side of the trail at mile 1.7. The formation stands alone and is easy to recognize. The hike ends at the south side of the parking area.

There is a proposed reroute for this trail in 2002. The new trail will be 2.6 miles and will include more of the maze.

USGS Topographical Map: Queen Mtn 7.5'   **Trail Map 20**

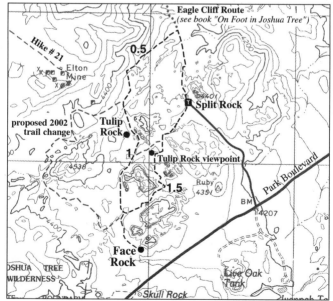

26 🔟 👣 🚶 Arch Rock

Highlights: interpretive trail, Arch Rock, large rock piles, side trip to White Tank
Mileage: 0.3 mile loop   **Time:** < 1 hour
Difficulty: easy   **Map:** Trail Map 21
Elevation Difference: minimal
Use Restrictions: day use only, no horses or bicycles
Access: White Tank Campground, near site #9

Description: Signs along this short nature trail explain the geology of the area and the natural creation of an arch. It took the forces of nature many years to create Arch Rock out of a monzogranite boulder pile. This arch spans a 35' distance and rises about 15' above the underlying boulder.

The trail travels to Arch Rock, circles through a rocky area, then exits near the end of the campground. Complete the loop by following the campground road back to the trailhead.

A short side trip (0.1 miles) through narrow alleys formed by rock monoliths leads to White Tank. In the early 1900's, cattlemen constructed this tank by building a small dam of rock and cement across the width of the wash. Rain run-off collected behind the wall and provided water for cattle. Like most of the other tanks in the park, White Tank has since filled with sand. However, just below the dam, there is a moist verdant area attractive to birds and wildlife. Above the tank, large boulders and natural crawlways fill the wash.

No trail leads to White Tank; the hike involves route finding and some rock scrambling. To find the tank, leave the trail at the Arch Rock exhibit sign and scramble up the boulders to the front of the arch. Continue past the arch through a narrow alley bordered by boulders on both sides. About 65 yards from the arch, the alley leads along the base of a large boulder

about 40' high. Scramble down through the alley past this boulder. Look left and find another large boulder with a passage under it. Climb through the passage to reach the top of the tank.

Arch Rock

USGS Topographical Map: Malapai Hill 7.5'   **Trail Map 21**

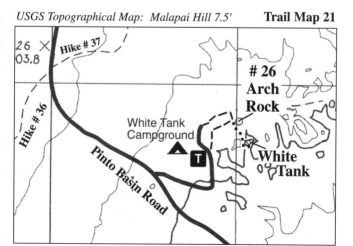

27 🖼 Cholla Cactus Garden

Highlights: interpretive trail, impressive dense collection of cholla
Mileage: 0.25 mile loop   **Time:** < 1 hour
Difficulty: easy   **Map:** unnecessary
Elevation Difference: relatively level
Use Restrictions: day use only, no horses or bicycles
Access: Cholla Parking Area. From the Pinto Wye road junction, drive 10 miles south on Pinto Basin Road. The parking lot is on the right (west) side of the road.

Description: This trail travels through an unusually dense concentration of Bigelow cholla, a plant characteristic to both the Mojave and the Colorado deserts. From a distance, the Bigelow cholla looks soft and fuzzy and hence has gained the name teddy bear cholla. However, a close look at this plant will reveal the true identity of the Bigelow. Fine bristles cover each plant, and each bristle has a microscopic barb on the exposed end. Even brushing lightly against a cholla can cause the spines to penetrate and stick to skin and clothing.

Cholla Cactus Garden sits on the lower edge of the transition zone between the Mojave and Colorado deserts. The Joshua trees of the Mojave Desert do not extend to this lower elevation. They have been replaced by an abundance of creosote, the predominate plant in the Colorado Desert.

This trail provides a place to examine and learn about the plant and animal life in the Colorado Desert. A self-guiding trail pamphlet is available at the start of the trail.

Chapter 5
Hikes Near Cottonwood Campground

Cottonwood Campground is the only Joshua Tree National Park campground in the Colorado Desert. All the other park campgrounds are in the Mojave Desert. The Colorado Desert, which predominates the southern and eastern half of the park, lies at an elevation generally less than 3000'.

While there are similarities between the Mojave and Colorado deserts, there are also distinct differences in the vegetation. There are no Joshua trees in the Colorado Desert; a variety of other trees have replaced them. Mesquite, palo verdes, and smoke trees flourish along many of the sandy washes. There is a greater variety and a more abundance of cacti and flowers in the Colorado Desert than in the Mojave. Cottonwood has some of the best spring wildflower displays in the park.

Cottonwood sits on the lower edge of the Pinto Basin. It is bordered by the Cottonwood Mountains to the southwest and Eagle Mountains to the east. Facilities at Cottonwood include a visitor center, picnic area, and a 62-site campground with running water and flush toilets. There is a campground fee. Only the three group sites can be reserved. The nearest town is Indio, about 30 miles away.

The easiest way to reach Cottonwood is from Interstate 10. The well-marked park exit is halfway between Indio and Desert Center. The campground and visitor center lie about seven miles north of the Interstate. You can also reach Cottonwood from the northern part of the park by driving south on Pinto Basin Road.

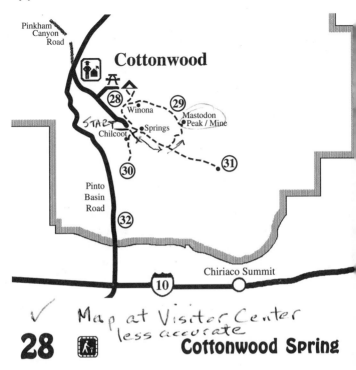

Pinkham Canyon Road

Cottonwood

28

Winona

29

Mastodon Peak / Mine

START

Springs

Chilcoot

30

31

Pinto Basin Road

32

Chiriaco Summit

10

✓ Map at Visitor Center
less accurate

28 🚶 Cottonwood Spring

Highlights: interpretive trail, Cottonwood Spring
Mileage: 1.4 miles (round-trip)   **Time:** 1 hour
Difficulty: easy   **Map:** Trail Map 22
Elevation Difference: 145'   **Total Uphill Travel:** 165'
Use Restrictions: day use only, no horses or bicycles
Access: Cottonwood Campground, sites 13A & 13B

Elevation Profile

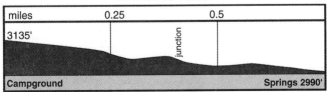

miles	0.25	0.5
3135'	junction	
Campground		Springs 2990'

Description: The Cottonwood Nature Trail provides an opportunity to explore the Colorado Desert and learn about its early human inhabitants. Long before the park was established, Cahuilla Indians inhabited the oases and springs in the southern park area. These people were well adapted to desert living. They thrived by making use of the many plants and animals of the Colorado Desert.

The Cottonwood Nature Trail passes through rolling hills as it travels from the campground to Cottonwood Spring. Signs along the trail interpret the plants and animals and explain how the Cahuilla Indians used the plants in their daily lives.

About 0.4 miles from the Loop B trailhead, there is a junction in a major wash. The nature trail leads to the right (west). Traveling to the left leads to the Winona Mill site (see hike #29). The nature trail ends at Cottonwood Spring. Return to the campground over the same trail.

Cottonwood Spring is a significant water source, sometimes producing up to 30 gallons an hour. The thick collection of palm trees and cottonwoods provides important habitat for wildlife in the area. The spring also proved to be an important water source for people between 1870 and 1910. It was one of the few water sources located along the popular route of travel between Mecca and the Dale Mining District. Pick up the park brochure entitled "A Day at Cottonwood Spring" to learn more about the area.

See #28 ALSO

29 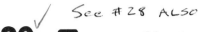 Mastodon Peak Loop

---

Highlights: Cottonwood Spring, historical sites, peak summit
Mileage: 2.5 mile loop   **Time:** 2 hours
Difficulty: moderate   **Map:** Trail Map 22
Elevation Difference: 370'   **Total Uphill Travel:** 396'
Use Restrictions: day use only, no horses or bicycles
Access: Cottonwood Spring Parking Area, at end of the paved
spur road that begins just south of Cottonwood Visitor Center

---

Elevation Profile

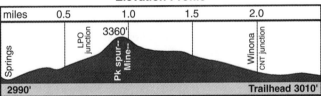

Description: The Mastodon Peak Loop travels past two sites
that were busy during the mining days. Traveling counter
clockwise from Cottonwood Spring, the trail passes Mastodon
Mine and then the Winona Mill site. The Mastodon Mine was
a gold mine that operated between 1919 and 1932. You can
still see the mine shafts today. (Do not enter mine shafts.
They are unstable and dangerous.)

Mastodon Peak (3440') lies just above the mine. Invite
your imagination to mimic that of the early prospectors who
named this peak. They imagined the rock formation, which
creates the peak, to be a likeness of a prehistoric elephant head.

Take a side trip to the top of Mastodon Peak. The impressive views from the peak include the Cottonwood area, Eagle
Peak, Monument Mountain, Mt. San Jacinto, Shavers Valley,
and the Salton Sea. Look for the marked trail junction around
mile 0.9 on the loop. From the junction, a rough, unmain-

tained trail leads 0.1 miles to the summit.   Although the climb is not difficult, it is narrow, exposed, and involves some rock scrambling.

Less than a mile past the Mastodon Mine lies Winona Mill. Winona was the site of a small village and mill that was active in the 1920's. Gold ore from the Mastodon Mine and other nearby mining claims was processed at this mill. The foundations of the mill buildings still dot the hillside. Cottonwoods and exotic trees and shrubs, which the millhands planted, flourish in a wash at the base of the hill. The large trees provide habitat for birds and wildlife and shade for passing hikers. The loop continues from Winona back to the Cottonwood Spring parking lot. See hike #28 for information on Cottonwood Spring.

USGS Topographical Map: Cottonwood Spring 7.5' **Trail Map 22**

30   Moorten's Mill / Little Chilcoot

Highlights: Cottonwood Spring, historical mining site, Little Chilcoot Pass, desert trees

Mileage: 1.2 miles (round-trip)   **Time:** 1 hour

Difficulty: easy   **Map:** Trail Map 22

Elevation Difference: 180'   **Total Uphill Travel:** 200'

Use Restrictions: day use only, no horses or bicycles

Access: Cottonwood Spring Parking Area, at end of the paved spur road that begins just south of Cottonwood Visitor Center

Description: A hike over the old teamster's route, and through a wash, leads to the site of a 5-stamp mill. "Cactus" Slim Moorten built the mill in the 1930's to process ore from his nearby claims.

The remains at the mill, which include a foundation, an old vehicle, and some rusted tanks, are meager. However, it is the route to the site, not the mill site itself, that makes this hike interesting. The route travels through a wash that is rich with Colorado Desert flora. Mesquite, palo verdes, smoke trees, and yuccas dominate the vegetation.

The teamster's route was the wagon road used to reach Cottonwood Spring in the early 1900's. The majority of the teamster's route has vanished. However, you can still see a short section of the road known as Little Chilcoot Pass. Little Chilcoot Pass was built to bypass a low cliff in the wash.

There is no trail for this hike, but wooden posts do mark the route. Follow the wash south from Cottonwood Spring. Travel over Little Chilcoot Pass, 1/4 mile from Cottonwood Spring, and continue down the wash to Moorten's Mill. The mill site is on the right side of the wash at the base of the hill. Watch for the wooden post with an arrow that points to the site.

31 🔟 🔺   Lost Palms Oasis

Highlights: Cottonwood Spring, oasis with 100+ palms, scenic canyon
Mileage: 7.5 miles (round-trip)   **Time:** 4 - 6 hours
Difficulty: moderately strenuous   **Map:** Trail Map 23
Elevation Difference: 460'   **Total Uphill Travel:** 1088'
Use Restrictions: partial day use, no horses or bicycles
Access: Cottonwood Spring Parking Area, at end of the paved spur road that begins just south of Cottonwood Visitor Center

Elevation Profile

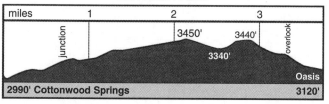

Description: Lost Palms Oasis is one of the largest palm oases in the park. There are more than 100 palms in the canyon. Beneath towering fan palms and rugged canyon walls, water trickles intermittently through a sandy wash then disappears in a boulder-clogged canyon below. The echoing of the canyon wren's song and the rustling of the palms add to the beauty of this remote area.

The trail to the oasis overlook travels through sandy washes and rolling hills. The overlook is the end of the "moderate" portion of the hike. A steep, rugged trail leads down to the oasis and canyon bottom. At the upper end of the oasis, there is a boulder-strewn side canyon that leads to Dike Springs and more palm stands.

Watch for animal tracks and droppings along the trail and in the canyon bottom. The combination of the water, rugged

terrain, and remoteness of the area makes Lost Palms Oasis ideal habitat for the elusive bighorn sheep. (See hike #5 for information about bighorn sheep.) Because the oasis is an important wildlife area, the National Park Service has designated it as a day use area. You can camp in the rolling hills before the overlook.

USGS Topographical Map: Cottonwood Spring 7.5′   **Trail Map 23**

*Towering palms and rocky canyon walls
dwarf a hiker at Lost Palms Oasis.*

32 🖼️♿ Bajada Nature Trail

Highlights: interpretive trail, all-access trail, low desert
Mileage: 0.25 mile loop   **Time:** < 1 hour
Difficulty: easy   **Map:** unnecessary
Elevation Difference: relatively level
Use Restrictions: day use only, no horses or bicycles
Access: parking lot on east side of Pinto Basin Road, 5.5 miles south of Cottonwood Visitor Center, 1.5 miles north of Interstate 10

Description: This hard-surfaced trail explores the natural life on a desert bajada. A bajada is a long slope composed of the eroded sand and gravel from nearby mountains. Signs along the trail interpret the plant and animal life of this bajada. Three benches spaced along the trail provide a place to relax and enjoy the area.

This trail was specially designed as an all-access trail for the physically impaired. The hard surface is appropriate for wheelchairs. For the visually impaired, there are raised tactile strips along the trail denoting the points of interest. An audio tape and tape deck, which you can borrow from the Cottonwood Visitor Center, explains these points of interest.

Chapter 6
California Riding & Hiking Trail

Thirty-seven miles of the California Riding and Hiking Trail traverse the park from Black Rock, in the westernmost part of the park, to the North Entrance near Twentynine Palms. As the trail travels from west to east, it passes through areas having distinct vegetation differences. It leads from the upper pinyon/juniper forests, through Joshua tree forests, to lower elevations where creosote is the predominant vegetation. You can hike the trail either in its entirety, which takes two to three days, or in shorter sections of 4.5 to 11.3 miles. In general, it is easier to travel from west to east since the western trail sections are at higher elevations.

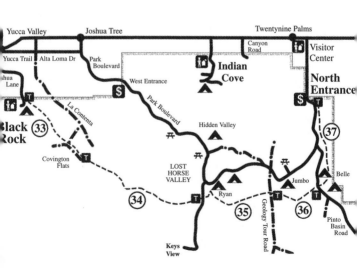

33 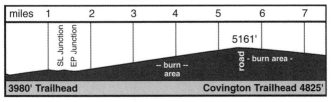 Black Rock to Covington Flats

Highlights: variety of high desert vegetation, interesting burn area, hike between mountains

Mileage: 7.6 miles (one-way)   **Time:** 3-5 hours

Difficulty: moderate   **Map:** Trail Map 24

Elevation Difference: 1205'   **Total Uphill Travel:** 1314'

Use Restrictions: no bicycles

Access: Black Rock Trailhead. Look for a large signboard on the east side of the road. It's just inside the Black Rock Campground entrance. There is limited parking at the trailhead; however, there is additional parking at the ranger station just up the road.

Finish: Covington Flats Trailhead. See Access for hike # 34.

Elevation Profile

miles	1	2	3	4	5	6	7

SL Junction
EP Junction
-- burn -- area
5161'
road - burn area -

3980' Trailhead   Covington Trailhead 4825'

Description: This trail leads gradually uphill from Black Rock to Covington Flats. (This is one segment of the California Riding and Hiking Trail that would be easier traveled from east to west.) The first section of the trail passes through hills over-looking Yucca Valley. Pinyon pines, junipers, and Joshua trees vegetate the area. The middle section travels up a sandy wash bordered by large hills. The final section of the hike parallels the Upper Covington Flats Road, a remote dirt road.

The trail passes through some areas that burned in the 1999 summer wildfires. The stark, eerie landscape, created by the burns, is particularly notable in the Upper Covington section. Black skeletons of Joshua trees, oaks, and chollas dot a

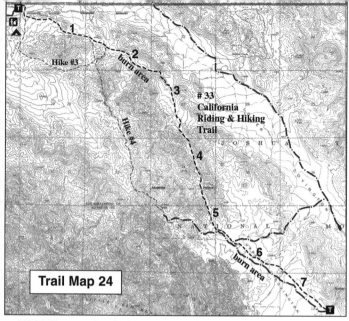

USGS Topographical Maps: Yucca Valley S., Joshua Tree South 7.5'

mostly brown landscape. There are a few splotchy areas of green annuals and only a few trees that were missed by the fire. Recovery from the fire in this area seems to be much slower than the area around Keys View Road (see hike #13). Compare the stark burn area to the last mile of the trail. The last mile travels through large Joshua trees and other vegetation untouched by the fire.

From the trailhead, hike a short distance east to a wide wash. Turn right and travel up the wash about 150 yards. At this point, the trail exits the wash to the left (east). A large sign identifies the California Riding and Hiking Trail. At mile 5.2 the trail reaches a dirt road that leads to Eureka Peak. Continue east on the trail and cross the Covington Road at mile 5.5. Continue the remaining two miles to the Covington Flats Trailhead. There are some faint trail sections particularly on the latter part of the hike. It would be wise to carry maps and a compass in case the trail markers are missing.

34 Covington Flats to Keys View Road

Highlights: variety of terrain, vegetation, and scenic views
Mileage: 11.3 miles (one-way)   **Time:** 5 - 7 hours
Difficulty: moderately strenuous   **Map:** Trail Map 25
Elevation Difference: 845'   **Total Uphill Travel:** 1166'
Use Restrictions: no bicycles
Access: Covington Flats Trailhead. Head east from Yucca Valley on Hwy 62. Turn right (south) on La Contenta Road. Cross Yucca Trail/Alta Loma and continue on a dirt road. Follow the dirt road to a junction on the left side (2.8 miles from Hwy 62). Watch for the "Covington Flats" sign. Turn left and continue 1.7 miles to the park boundary. Continue an additional 4.2 miles past the boundary to a junction. Turn right. Continue to another junction and turn left. Follow the road to the end.
Finish: Juniper Flats Trailhead. See Access for hike #35.

Elevation Profile

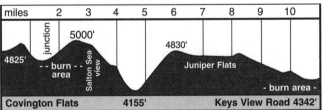

Description: Of the five California Riding & Hiking Trail sections, this section has the greatest variety of terrain, vegetation, and scenic views. The largest known Joshua tree in the park is 0.2 miles from the trailhead. The tree stands about thirty-five feet high and has a circumference of about seventeen feet at the base. Unfortunately the tree has started to deteriorate in the last few years. It has lost many branches and some bark from its base. (Please help prolong the tree's life

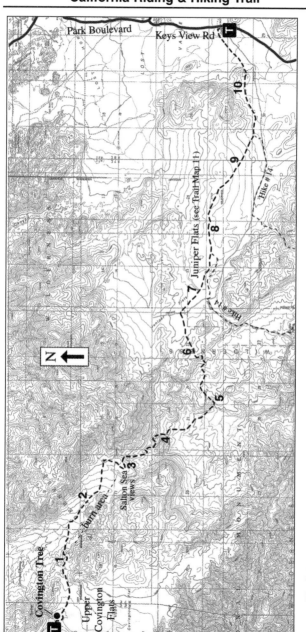

USGS Topographical Maps: Joshua Tree South, East Deception Canyon, Keys View 7.5'

Trail Map 25

by not climbing on it.) The trail travels past this tree and through more large Joshua trees.

Farther on, the trail winds around a hillside through thicker vegetation—juniper, pinyon pine, and jojoba. A few switchbacks lead down the hillside to a flat valley that burned over in the 1999 summer wildfires. Distant Mt. San Gorgonio rises above this valley. The trail continues up out of the valley to a plateau then travels along a high ridge. From the ridge, the view of the Salton Sea is excellent. A rocky trail descends the ridge, travels along a lower hillside, then zigzags up to Juniper Flats. Tracks and droppings indicate the elusive bighorn sheep frequent this area. (Note: A few short trail sections may be difficult to follow. Look for cairns or rock piles that mark the route through the washes and burn areas and over rocky terrain.)

Juniper Flats (see hike #13) is another highlight of this hike. Large juniper trees abound in this scenic, relatively level area. At Juniper Flats, the trail crosses a dirt road (closed to vehicles) then continues gradually downhill the remaining 4.5 miles to Keys View Road. This last portion of the trail follows along a ridge that offers excellent views of the Wonderland.

The largest known Joshua tree in the park

35 ▲🐎 Keys View Road to Geology Tour Road

Highlights: mining camp ruins, Joshua trees, mountain pass
Mileage: 6.6 miles (one-way)   **Time:** 3-4 hours
Difficulty: moderate   **Map:** Trail Map 26
Elevation Difference: 210'   **Total Uphill Travel:** 424'
Use Restrictions: no bicycles
Access: Juniper Flats Trailhead. Drive one mile south of Park Boulevard on Keys View Road. The parking lot is on the right (west) side of the road.
Finish: Geology Tour Road. See Access for hike #36.

Elevation Profile

miles	1	2	3	4	5	6

LOST HORSE VALLEY   Ryan Camp   4550'   mining camp   QUEEN VALLEY   4493'

4342' Keys View Rd   4345'   Geology Tour Road

Description: This trail travels over a low pass between Ryan and Lost Horse mountains. The trail leads gradually up from Lost Horse Valley to the pass then down the other side into Queen Valley. East of the pass, the trail travels by a horizontal mine shaft (unsafe for entry) located thirty feet to the right of the trail. Look for the remains of a prospector camp located a short distance beyond the mine and on the opposite side of the trail.

This is just one of the many mining camp ruins found throughout the park. A few lucky and industrious desert pioneers did discover rich deposits of gold as shown by the success of the Lost Horse and Desert Queen mines (see hikes #15 & #22). However, most pioneer prospectors were hardly able to scrape out a meager existence. Ruins, such as this one, are

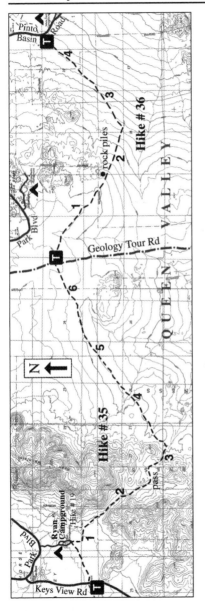

all that remain of their unfulfilled dreams of gold and great wealth.

From the ruins, the trail continues across Queen Valley to the Geology Tour Road.

You can also access the trail from Ryan Campground. Starting from the campground shortens the hike by 0.8 miles.

Trail Map 26

USGS Topographical Maps: Keys View, Malapai Hill 7.5'

36 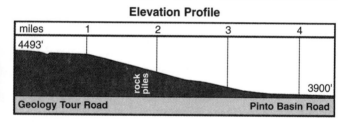 Geology Tour Road to Pinto Basin Road

---

Highlights: southern scenic views, rock piles

Mileage: 4.5 miles (one-way)   **Time:** 2-3 hours

Difficulty: easy   **Map:** Trail Map 26

Elevation Difference: 593'   **Total Uphill Travel:** 10'

Use Restrictions: no bicycles

Access: Geology Tour Road. Drive 1.4 miles south of Park Boulevard on Geology Tour Road. The parking lot is on the left (east) side of the road.

Finish: Twin Tanks Trailhead. See Access for hike #37.

Elevation Profile

miles	1	2	3	4

4493'

rock piles

3900'

Geology Tour Road   **Pinto Basin Road**

Description: This is the shortest and easiest section of the California Riding & Hiking Trail. It travels gradually downhill as it leads from west to east across Queen Valley. About 1.7 miles from Geology Tour Road, the trail passes near large rock formations. The rocks provide a scenic and sheltered place to camp or have lunch. The remainder of the trail travels through the open valley where there are good views of two outstanding and unique areas in the park—Pinto Basin and the distant Coxcomb Mountains. (See map on page 4.)

Pinto Basin is an immense basin measuring close to 200 square miles. It is mostly untouched by road or human foot. Although two roads do travel through parts of the area, most of the basin remains a wilderness.

Beyond Pinto Basin is the Coxcomb Mountain Range, a wilderness of remote, highly distinctive, rugged peaks. Due to its inaccessibility, this range has become a sanctuary for desert bighorn sheep. The sheep roam at ease, but in limited numbers, through this isolated maze of mountains.

37  Pinto Basin Road to North Entrance

Highlights: rock piles, Bull's Eye Rock
Mileage: 7.3 miles (one-way)   **Time:** 3-4 hours
Difficulty: easy   **Map:** Trail Map 27
Elevation Difference: 1060'   **Total Uphill Travel:** 76'
Access: Twin Tanks Trailhead. Drive 2.2 miles south of Park Boulevard on Pinto Basin Road or 27.5 miles north of Cottonwood Visitor Center. The parking lot is on the west side of the road.
Finish: North Entrance Trailhead. Drive 1/2 mile south of the North Entrance Station to a dirt road junction on the east side of Park Boulevard. Drive to the end of the short dirt road.

Elevation Profile

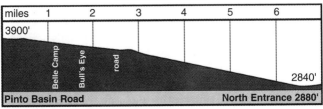

Description: The final section of the California Riding & Hiking Trail is almost all downhill. The trail parallels the road its entire length, although it is far enough removed to obscure the sound of motors. The most interesting part of the trail is the first three miles. This section travels along the base of Belle

Mountain and through rock piles located east of Belle Campground.

Look for an interesting rock formation, appropriately named Bull's Eye Rock, at mile 1.8. From the correct angle, Bull's Eye Rock looks like a giant calf's head. The eye is a perfectly round hole through the rock. By itself, the eye appears like a giant shotgun slug hole. Locate the formation by finding a rock pile that sits a few feet off the trail's east side. The Bull's Eye is just behind and northeast of this rock pile.

From mile 3 to the end, the trail travels through or adjacent to a wash. The trail is prone to washouts; carry a topographical map and compass in case you lose the trail.

This trail is one of the few hiking trails designated as a mountain bike trail. However, due to its sandy nature, it is only recommended for expert bikers. Additional caution is due as there are large chollas on the side of the trail. An error in maneuvering at the wrong time could have disastrous results.

Trail Map 27

USGS Topographical Maps: Malapai Hill, Queen Mtn. 7.5'

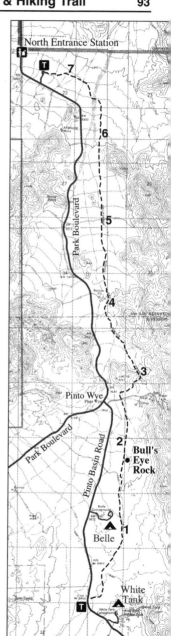

Mileage Chart
(Includes mileage start to finish)

Easy Hikes

#	Hike	Miles	Hours	🔟	👥	🥾	⛺	🐎	🚲
16	Keys View	0.25	<1		•				
27	Cholla Garden	0.25	<1		•				
32	Bajada Trail	0.25	<1		•				
26	Arch Rock	0.3	<1	•	•	•			
18	Cap Rock	0.4	<1		•	•			
8	Oasis of Mara	0.5	<1		•				
5	Indian Cove	0.6	<1		•				
10	Hidden Valley	1	1	•	•	•			
19	Ryan Homestead	1	1			•		•	
30	Moorten's Mill	1.2	1						
11	Barker Dam	1.4	1	•	•	•			
28	Cottonwood Spring	1.4	1		•				
24	Skull Rock	1.65	1		•	•			
12	Wonderland Wash	2	1.5	•		•			
25	Split Rock Loop	2	1-2			•		•	
21	Lucky Boy Vista	2.5	2			•	•		
23	Pine City	3	2			•	•		•
36	CA Riding & Hiking Geology Tour Road - Pinto Basin Road *	4.5	2-3			•	•		
37	CA Riding & Hiking Pinto Basin Road - North Entrance *	7.3	3-4			•	•		•

one-way hikes

Moderate Hikes

#	Hike	Miles	Hours	10	👣	🥾	⛺	🐴	🚲
2	South Park Peak	0.7	<1		•	•			
1	High View	1.3	1		•				
22	Desert Queen Mine	1.5	1.5			•			
29	Mastodon Loop	2.5	2			•			
3	Short Loop	4	2-3				•	•	
15	Lost Horse Mine	4	2-3				•	•	
35	CA Riding & Hiking Keys View Road - Geology Tour Rd *	6.6	3-4				•	•	
33	CA Riding & Hiking Black Rock-Covington *	7.6	3-5				•	•	
6	Boy Scout Trail *	8	4-5				•	•	
13	Juniper Flats	9	4-6				•	•	

Moderately Strenuous Hikes

#	Hike	Miles	Hours	10	👣	🥾	⛺	🐴	🚲
17	Inspiration Peak	1.4	1.5	•					
7	49 Palms Oasis	3	2-3	•		•			
20	Ryan Mountain	3	2-3	•			•		
4	Eureka Peak *	5	3-4				•	•	
9	North View / Maze / Window Rock Loop	6.6	4-6	•			•	•	
31	Lost Palms Oasis	7.5	4-6	•			•		
34	CA Riding & Hiking Covington-Keys View *	11.3	5-7				•	•	
14	Stubbe Spring Loop	12	6-8	•			•	•	

About the Author

Patty Knapp is an outdoor writer and hiking enthusiast. She has written several hiking guides and park related children's books. She brings more than ten years of experience as a National Park Service Ranger to her writing, which includes three years at Joshua Tree National Park. It's this first hand working experience that adds insightful substance to her books.

Patty regularly returns to Joshua Tree to maintain her research and continue her explorations. She worked closely with National Park Service employees to insure that the information in this guide is as up-to-date and accurate as possible.

Other books by Patty Knapp and M. I. Adventure Publications

www.blissnet.com/~miap

On Foot in Joshua Tree National Park: A comprehensive hiking guide to Joshua Tree National Park that includes more than 100 hikes. Hikes include trails as well as an extensive selection of trailless routes to mountain summits and other highlights. The book includes over 40 photographs and illustrations, a selection of color topographic maps, and reference charts. Introductory pages feature the history and natural aspects of the park as well as general park information.

Getting to Know Joshua Tree National Park: An informative family guide to Joshua Tree National Park that features large full-color photographs. The book covers the highlights of the park, flora, fauna, geology, history, and recreational activities. The large map with mileage chart is helpful for planning a trip. For children and young adults, there are activities, stories, checklists, and a fold-out scenic poster.

Getting to Know Yellowstone National Park: A family guide to Yellowstone National Park.

Ranger Ray's Campfire Story: A children's coloring storybook.